Blender 2.8 for techni

Render 2D drawings for architecture,

Allan Brito

Description and data

Technical info about the Book

Author: Allan Brito

Reference: blender3darchitect.com

Edition: 1st

Cover image credits: danist @Unsplash

Licensed in public domain - https://unsplash.com/license

Blender version used in the Book: 2.81 Beta

First edition date: November 2019

ISBN: 9781709481710

Imprint: Independently published

About the author

Allan Brito is a Brazilian architect that has a passion for applying technology and open source to design and visualization. He is a longtime Blender user ever since 2005 and believes the software can become a great player in the architecture and design markets.

You will find more about him and the use of Blender for architecture in **blender3darchitect.com**, where he writes articles about the subject daily.

Who should read this book?

The book has a direct approach on how to create technical drawings with Blender 2.8 and will even list all the steps necessary to perform some tasks. No prior experience with Blender is required to follow the chapters. In the first chapter, we cover all the fundamental aspects of Blender necessary to start making technical drawings.

If you are looking for a way to create technical drawings with free software that is also capable of creating animations and realists render, this book is for you.

Foreword

When you think about Blender and what it can produce, you will probably start to think about animations, 3D models for games, and also realistic renderings with Cycles. But, what if I could you that it can also produce technical drawings?

In Blender, you will find a vast range of options regarding creative tools to produce all types of graphics and animations. One of those tools will allow you to render technical drawings using even a vector format. For professionals that want to use a tool to create a design or floor plan quickly, Blender 2.8 offers all the options and tools to support such creations.

The technical drawing capabilities will use FreeStyle as the primary option to produce 2D renderings from models that have all the shapes and settings from a technical drawing. You will add dimension lines, annotations, and even technical symbols. From the technical drawings produced in Blender, you can quickly create 3D models later using the 2D drawings as a base for future models. The possibilities are endless with such a technique.

If you want to expand your creative options with Blender and also fill the gap between your artistic and technical drawing needs, the book will help you find the best techniques and solutions to render technical drawings. By using those techniques, you will be able to integrate Blender even more in a design workflow.

I hope you like the book and find the content useful for your personal and professional needs.

Allan Brito

Downloading Blender

One of the significant advantages of Blender when comparing to similar softwares is their open-source nature. You can use Blender without any hidden costs! All you have to do is download the software and start using it.

How to download it? To download Blender, you should visit the Blender Foundation website:

`https://www.blender.org/download/`

For this book, we will use version *2.81 Beta of Blender*, but the vast majority of techniques will still work with later versions.

Download book files

You can download the Blender files used in the book in the following address:

`https://www.blender3darchitect.com/b28techdrawing`

All files use Blender 2.81. The ZIP file will include:

- **Base files used during chapter development**: Look for a file name identifying each chapter
- **Finished files with all settings for rendering**: Look for a file name with FINAL

Intentionally left blank

TABLE OF CONTENTS

Intentionally left blank

Chapter 1 - Blender basics for technical drawing

If you are getting to use Blender for the first time to produce technical drawings, we will start the first chapter of the book with an overview of how Blender works and what you need to know to start making 2D drawings. The primary objective of this chapter is to give you the tools and knowledge necessary to feel comfortable with Blender.

From the user interface to the shortcuts used to manipulate the scene and also some basic options to create and edit objects. A vital component of any attempt to dram 2D shapes in Blender is to manipulation of your 3D Viewport. The chapter describes how you can create an orthographic view from a scene that later will become a technical drawing.

If you already have some basic knowledge about Blender, you might skip this chapter and go straight to Chapter 2 to start rendering 2D drawings.

Here is a list of what you will learn:

– How to start with Blender for technical drawing

– Navigation and selection shortcuts

– Using orthographic views for technical drawing

– Drawing objects in 2D

– Precision drawing options and units settings

– Shading modes for 2D drawing

1.1 Starting with Blender for technical drawing

The first time you open Blender after the installation process, you will have to make an important choice, which will affect the way you use Blender to create technical drawings or any other project. At the Quick Setup window, you will be able to choose what types of shortcuts you want to use, and also the mouse button used for selection (Figure 1.1).

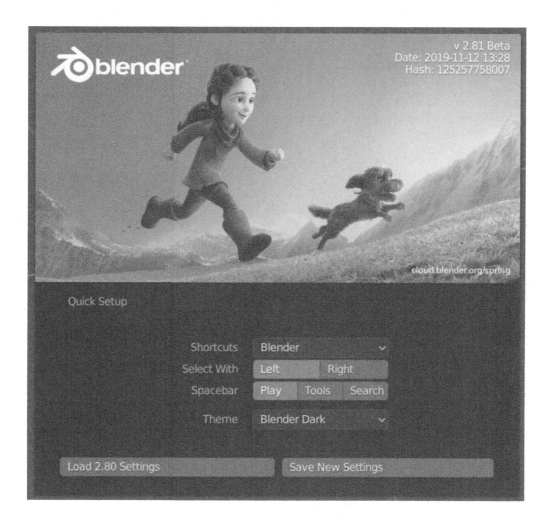

Figure 1.1 - Quick Setup

From the shortcuts list, you can pick three main options:

– Blender

- Blender 2.7X

- Industry compatible

Besides the shortcuts, you can also choose the button used for selection. Until Blender 2.7x, we had the right mouse button as the default option. That is the opposite of all other 3D applications. The new default for Blender 2.8x is the left mouse button.

Across the book, we will use the left mouse button for selection and all shortcuts with Blender defaults. Unless you want to make changes to the settings, you will use the default options for the Quick Setup.

Click anywhere outside of the Quick Setup window to start using Blender. Then, you will see the default user interface for Blender (Figure 1.2).

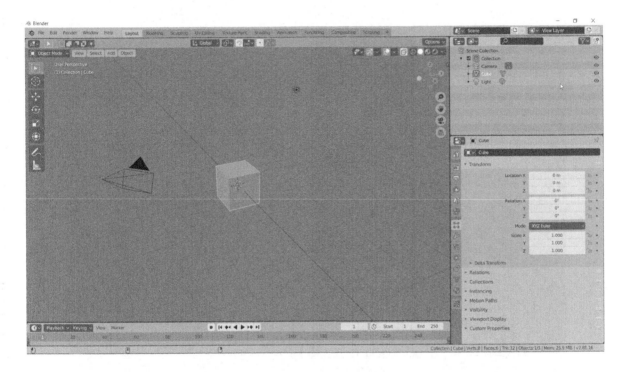

Figure 1.2 - Default used interface

From the interface, you will notice it has several divisions like the large 3D space at the center that has a Cube. That Editor has the name of 3D Viewport and is the place where we will create all 3D objects. Besides the 3D Viewport you will also have:

- Timeline Editor

- Outline Editor

14

– Properties Editor

Each one of those Editors will work for a different purpose (Figure 1.3).

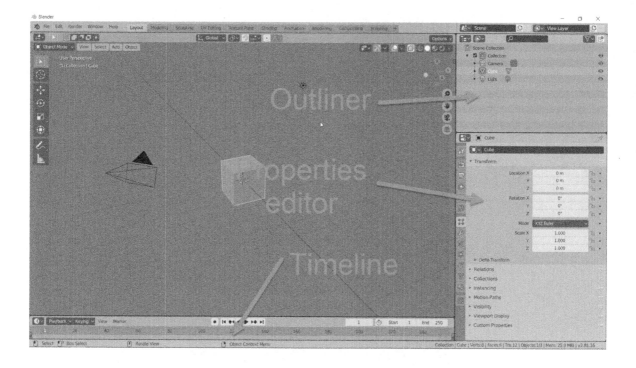

Figure 1.3 - *Blender editors*

Regarding technical drawing creation in Blender, we will mostly use the Properties Editor to make changes to settings related to rendering, materials, and also stroke rendering for 3D objects. We will also use the Outliner Editor to control and manage Collections on several occasions.

It is possible to resize and adjust the Editor's size by placing the mouse cursor at the border of each Editor. When it turns into a double side arrow, you can click and drag the border to resize (Figure 1.4).

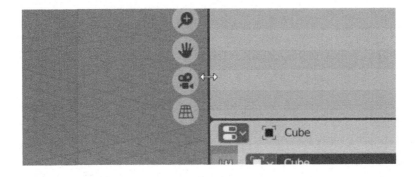

Figure 1.4 - *Resize editors*

You can also split the Editors area with a right-click on the border, which will open the Area Options menu (Figure 1.5).

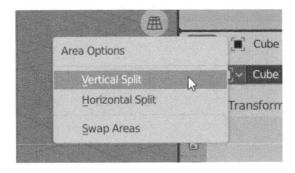

Figure 1.5 - *Area Options*

There you will find options to organize the user interface with:

– **Vertical split**: Makes a vertical division from the same border

– **Horizontal split**: Create a horizontal division from the same border

– **Swap Areas**: Interchange the editors that share the same border

To merge two editors, you will have to click and drag from the borders of a window. The mouse cursor will turn into a cross, which you will click and drag to another editor. A large arrow appears to help you visualize the direction of a merge. Only editors that share the same border are eligible for a merge.

It is also possible to change the Editor type using the selector available in each editor header (Figure 1.6).

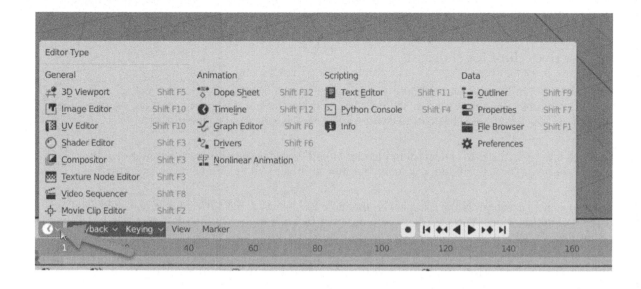

Figure 1.6 - *Editor selection*

What Editors will we need to create technical drawings? For technical drawing creation you will need the following editors:

– 3D Viewport

– Properties Editor

– Outliner Editor

– Compositor

Since most of the required editors are available in the default user interface, you don't have to make any changes to the editors for technical drawing creation.

You can also use WorkSpaces to change the arrangement of your editors for a certain task. At the top of your 3D Viewport, you will see several tabs like:

– Layout

– Modeling

– Sculpting

– UV Editing

Clicking at any of those tabs will change the interface layout to help you with a task. Later in the book, we will use the Compositing WorkSpace to mix View Layers from Blender in chapter 6.

For now, you should keep using the Layout tab.

1.1.1 Active editor for shortcuts

Besides editors in Blender, you will also have to become familiar with keyboard shortcuts that can save you an incredible amount of time in 3D modeling and also technical drawing creation. Across the book, we will use several of those shortcuts to create objects and also manipulate the project.

When you press a key to call a tool in Blender, it will consider something called "Active Editor" to apply the shortcut. The active Editor is where your mouse cursor is at the moment you press the key.

For instance, if you press the E key when the mouse cursor is at the 3D Viewport, you will call the Extrude tool in Edit Mode. The same key has a different function at the Outliner Editor. There it will enable or disable a Collection.

From this point forward, you should consider the Editor in which we are working every time we pass instructions to press a certain key. Otherwise, you may have a completely different tool called from that shortcut.

1.2 Navigation and selection shortcuts

A key element in the technical drawing creation is the ability to manipulate the 3D Viewport of Blender by changing the zoom and visualization of a project. You can use the mouse and keyboard to manage the 3D Viewport with the following shortcuts:

- **Middle mouse button**: Press the button and move the mouse to start rotating your view.
- **SHIFT+ Middle mouse button**: Press the keys and drag your mouse to move your screen (Pan).
- **CTRL+Middle mouse button**: Press both keys and move your mouse up and down for zoom in and out.
- **Mouse wheel**: Zoom in and out from the scene.
- **Home key**: Zoom all objects in your scene

Besides the shortcuts, you can also use the icons located at the top right corner of your 3D Viewport (Figure 1.7).

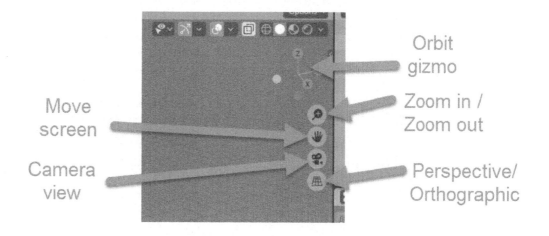

Orbit gizmo

Move screen

Zoom in / Zoom out

Camera view

Perspective/ Orthographic

Figure 1.7 - Navigation icons

As for the selection of objects, you will use the left mouse button to select any objects in your 3D Viewport. For instance, you can click at the objects, and you will see an orange outline at the object (Figure 1.8).

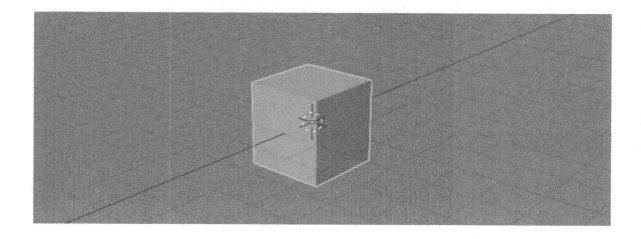

Figure 1.8 - Selected object

To select multiple objects, you can hold the SHIFT key and left-click on various objects to add them to the selection. To remove all objects from selection, press the ALT+A keys.

A quick way to select multiple objects in Blender is with the B key that will enable you to draw a box, which will add all objects inside that area to the selection. You can either press the B key to start that selection or use the icons from the 3D Viewport toolbar to use multiple selection modes (Figure 1.9).

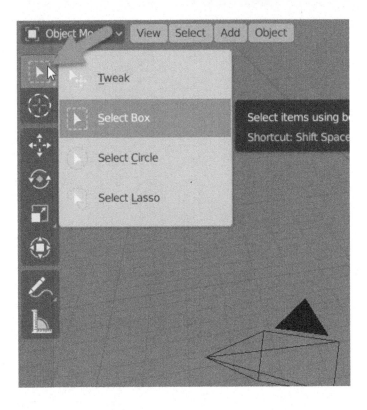

Figure 1.9 - *Selection modes*

There you can enable options like the Select Box, Select Circle, and Lasso Select. With the Toolbar, we can access multiple options related to object edition and manipulation in Blender. Using the T key in your 3D Viewport enables and disables that sidebar.

Another vital selection shortcut in Blender is the A key that will select all objects in the active Editor. The selection shortcuts in Blender works across multiple editors, and you will be able to apply them regardless of the active Editor you have at the moment.

Tip: A useful shortcut for object selection is the CTRL+I that inverts the current selection. Using that key will enable you to invert any selection quickly. For instance, you can start selecting one object and press CTRL+I to remove that object from the selection and get all other objects.

1.3 Orthographic views for technical drawing

To work with technical drawing creation in Blender, we have to use orthographic projections in the rendering and also the drawing stages. Since Blender is a 3D environment, you can use either a perspective or orthographic projection for your 3D Viewport. At the 3D Viewport you can use the following shortcuts:

– **Numpad 5**: Swap between orthographic and perspective projections.

- **Numpad 1**: Front view

- **Numpad 3**: Right view

- **Numpad 7**: Top view

If you press the CTRL key alongside each one of the Numpad 1, 3, and 7, you will get the opposite view. For instance, you will get the Left View pressing the CTRL+Numpad 3 keys.

For instance, you can press the Numpad 7 in the 3D Viewport to see your project from the top (Figure 1.10).

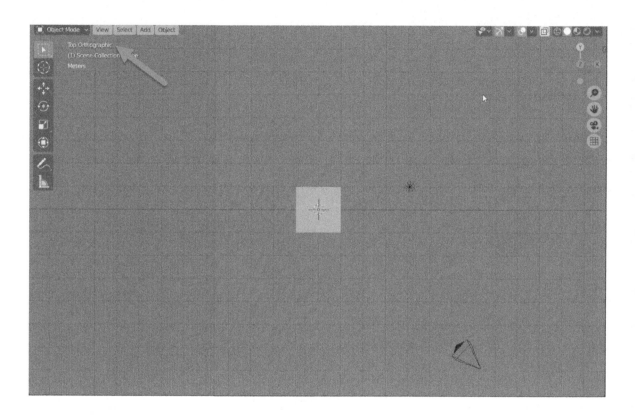

Figure 1.10 - Top view

Notice how you will see the name of your current projection at the top left corner. You can also use the Orbit Gizmo to change your view. Click at any one of the circles from the gizmo to change your view. Using the circle with the Z inside will give you the top view.

Another important shortcut that you might need to set up an environment for technical drawing is Numpad 5. That key will swap the projection from orthographic to perspective.

21

What if you are using a computer that doesn't have a numeric keyboard (Numpad)? In that case, we will have to enable an option from the User Preferences to emulate the Numpad. Go to the Edit → Preferences menu and look for the Input tab (Figure 1.11).

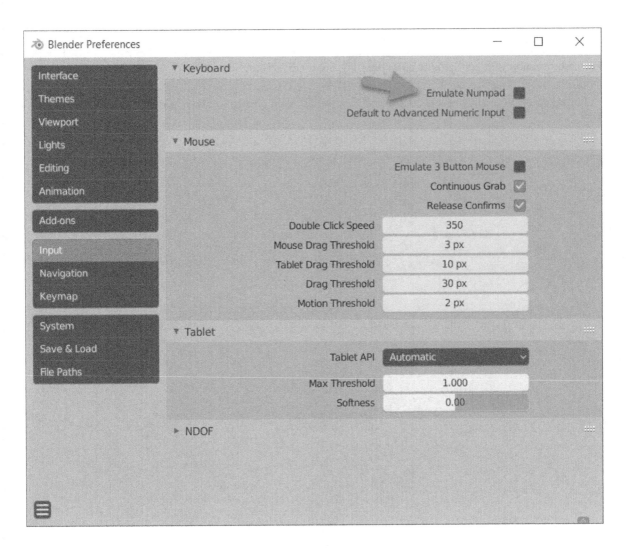

Figure 1.11 - Emulate Numpad

There you can enable the "Emulate Numpad" option, and your numeric keys from the alphanumeric keyboard will work as if there were from the Numpad.

1.3.1 Cameras for technical drawing

All the technical drawings we produce in Blender will require a render to create the visual output. Regardless of the method and format you choose for the output, everything will need a render. You can render your projects in Blender using the F12 key.

Before we start working with the rendering of technical drawings, it is necessary to understand how cameras work in Blender. Because every time you render anything in Blender, only what the active camera is viewing will appear at the render.

What is the camera? If you look to the objects at the default scene of Blender, you will see an object that has a pyramidal shape (Figure 1.12).

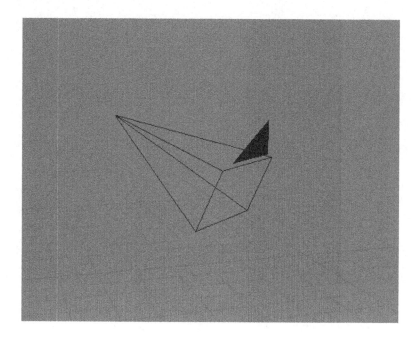

Figure 1.12 - *Camera object*

That is a camera object in Blender, which you will have to manipulate to adjust the render. For instance, if you press F12 at the default scene, you will see an image that looks like Figure 1.13.

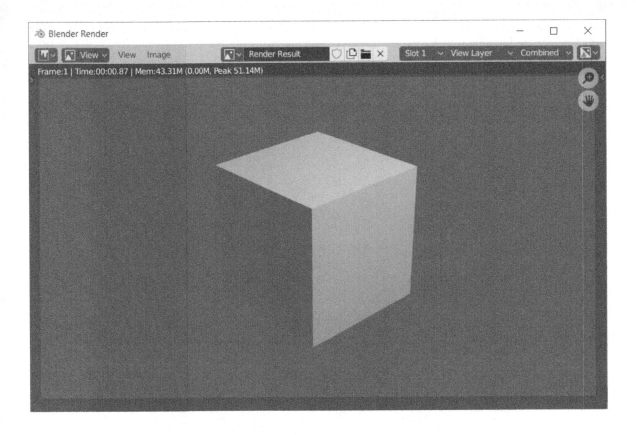

Figure 1.13 - Render from default camera

How to make the camera view the scene from the top? If you press the Numpad 7 key, only the current view will change, but not the camera. You can align the camera to the top view using a shortcut. Here is the procedure:

1. Press the Numpad 7

2. Use the navigation and zoom keys to align the Cube to the window center

3. Press the CTRL+ALT+Numpad 0

If you press those keys in sequence, you will get the camera aligned to the top view. You can replace step 3 by the **View → Align View → Align Camera** to View menu. Press the F12 key to render again, and you will see the object from the top.

The camera is viewing the scene from the top, but it doesn't have an orthographic projection. You can change that by selecting the camera object by clicking at the border (Figure 1.14).

Figure 1.14 - *Selecting the camera*

With the camera selected, you can open the Object Data Properties tab. That field will always show options related to the selected object in your Properties Editor. There you can change camera type to Orthographic (Figure 1.15).

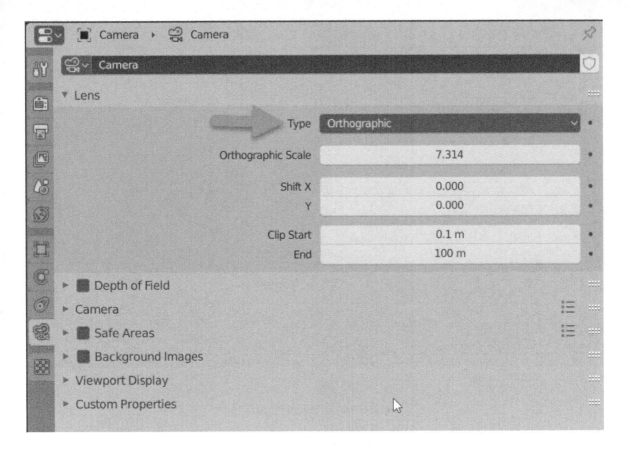

Figure 1.15 - Camera type

Use the value below your Type selector called "Orthographic Scale" to adjust the zoom of your camera. Pressing the F12 key will render an orthographic view from the top.

With the camera selected, you can also adjust the framing of your visualization using transformation shortcuts. We will learn more about those shortcuts in section 1.4.1.

1.4 Drawing objects in 2D for technical drawing

How to create 2D objects in Blender for technical drawing? Despite what you might think about Blender, it doesn't have any special mode to create 2D objects for technical drawings. We will create 3D objects using only two dimensions and render them with an orthographic projection.

The output result will be a 2D image projection that we can format as if it was a technical drawing coming from any CAD tool. Since we will create 2D objects for technical drawings, we will start the drawing process by removing the default cube. Select the Cube and press either the X or DELETE keys.

To create a new object, we will use the SHIFT+A keys, which will open a floating menu with all the creation options (Figure 1.16).

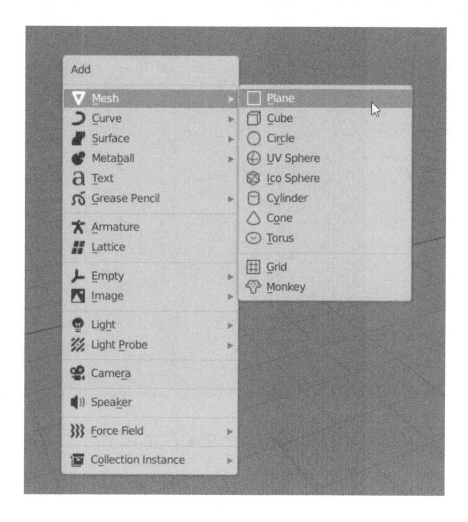

Figure 1.16 - *Creation options*

For technical drawing, in general, you should prefer to use either the **Mesh → Plane** or **Mesh → Circle**. Both objects already appear in the 3D Viewport as bidimensional shapes.

An important concept about creating objects in Blender is that all of them will always appear at the same location as your 3D Cursor. The 3D Cursor is a small crosshair symbol that has multiple used in Blender (Figure 1.17).

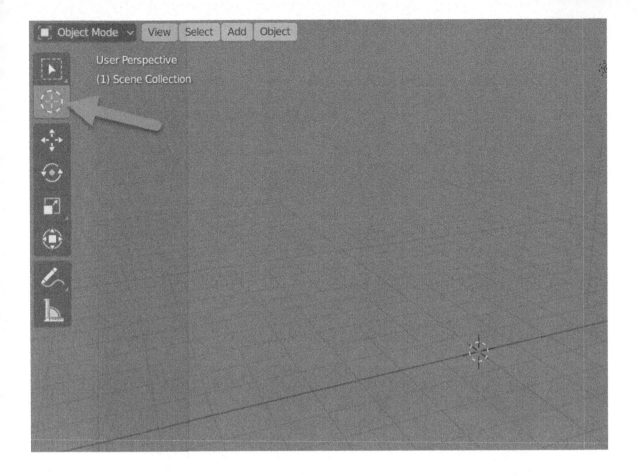

Figure 1.17 - *3D Cursor*

To move your 3D Cursor around, you can either hold the SHIFT key and right-click anywhere in your 3D Viewport or use the 3D Cursor button from the Toolbar.

There are other ways to place and control the cursor location like we will discuss later in the book. For instance, you can use the SHIFT+S keys to align the Cursor with any object using the Snap.

Tip: Use the SHIFT+C keys to reset your 3D Cursor location to the origin of the scene.

1.4.1 Using Edit Mode for drawing

After you create an object like a plane at the 3D Cursor location, it is time to start making a 2D drawing. In Blender, you will find something called work modes. At the moment, we are in Object Mode, as you can see from the work mode selector (Figure 1.18).

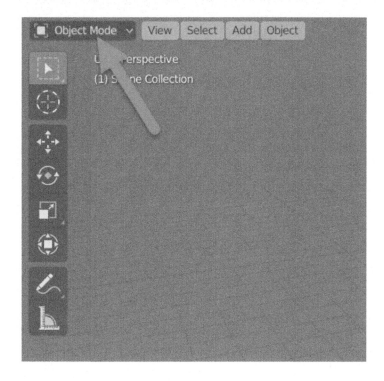

Figure 1.18 - *Work Mode Selector*

The mode we need to make 2D drawings based on 3D objects has the name of Edit Mode. You can either click at the selector to activate Edit Mode or press the TAB key. As a result of going to Edit Mode, you can view and manipulate the structure of 3D polygons.

A Mesh object in Blender is a 3D Polygon that has three main selectable parts:

– Vertices

– Edges

– Faces

The first time you go to Edit Mode, it will use the selection mode set to vertex. But, you can change the mode to any other element with the three buttons right next to the work mode selector (Figure 1.19).

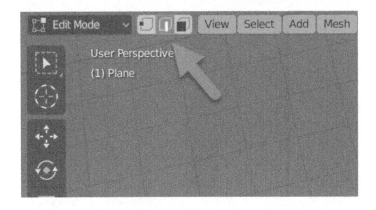

Figure 1.19 - Selection mode

You can use the same shortcuts and options to select the individual parts of any 3D object.

Info: Notice how the Toolbar changes in Edit Mode and shows a lot more options related to 3D modeling.

1.4.2 Duplicating an element or object

With any object or element from a polygon selected, you can quickly make a copy of that object pressing the SHIFT+D keys. For instance, you can select the edge of an object and press the SHIFT+D. The shortcut will create a copy of the object and immediately start a move transformation (Figure 1.20).

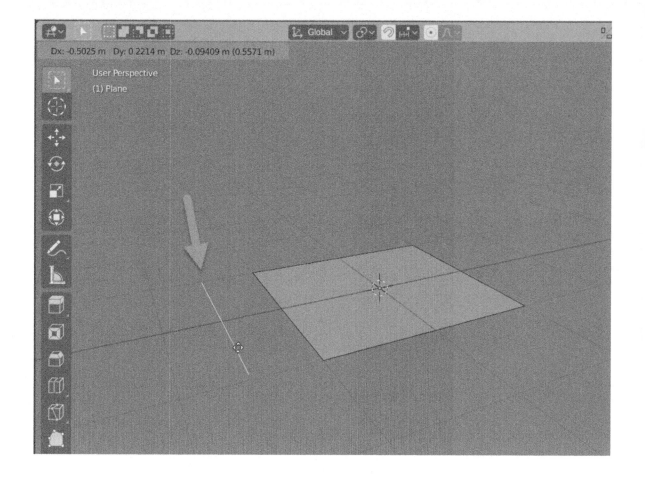

Figure 1.20 - *Duplicating an edge*

You must left-click anywhere to confirm the position for the copied object. The shortcut will work on both Object Mode to duplicate an entire object or only a segment.

1.4.3 Object transformation

To transform objects in Blender, we have a few options that you will have to know before starting making any 2D drawing. You can apply a transformation using the buttons available at the Toolbar (Figure 1.21).

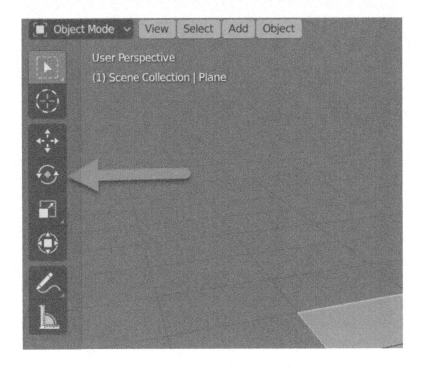

Figure 1.21 - *Transform options*

There are three main transformation types:

– Move

– Rotate

– Scale

For each transformation you have a button at the Toolbar, and also a keyboard shortcut:

– **G Key**: Move

– **R key**: Rotate

– **S key**: Scale

To work with precision modeling for technical drawing you should always try to use the shortcuts because they allow the use of numeric input. Besides the numeric input, we can also press a key corresponding to the axis you want to use for that transformation.

For instance, you can press the G key to start moving an object and right after press the X key. It will move the selected element or object only on the X-axis.

For instance, you can select an edge from a plane (Figure 1.22).

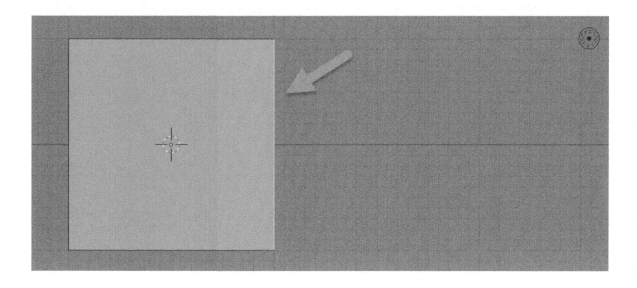

Figure 1.22 - *Selected edge*

With that edge selected:

1. Press the G key

2. Press the X key

3. Type 3

4. Press RETURN to confirm

By following this sequence of keys, will you move the edge three units in the X-axis. The resulting axis will go to the right, and by using a negative value, the edge would go to the left (Figure 1.23).

Figure 1.23 - *Moving an edge*

The same applies to all other transformations where the rotation will use degrees for input and the scale a factor that starts with 1 for 100% of the object size.

1.4.4 Drawing with the extrude

Regarding 2D drawing in Blender, there is a tool that will help you a lot in the creation process of shapes for technical drawing. With the extrude tool, you can select a single or multiple elements in Edit Mode and create a derivate shape.

To use the extrude tool, you can either press the corresponding button at the Toolbar or use the E key with an element selected (Figure 1.24).

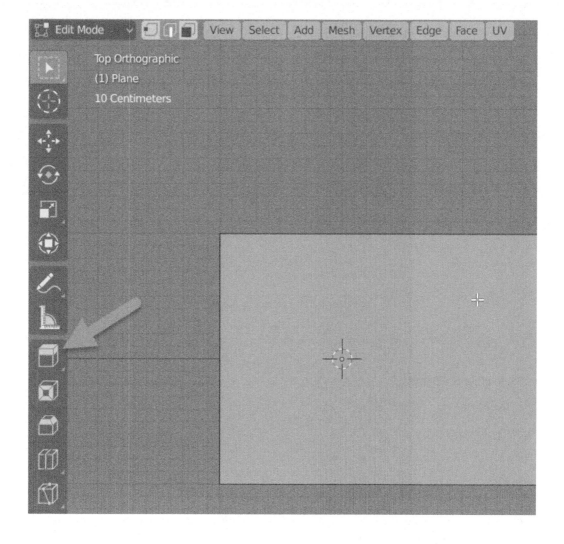

Figure 1.24 - *Extrude button*

You can draw with the extrude by selecting an edge or vertices from any 2D shape you have at the scene. Press the E key to start extruding them, and you will be able to make new shapes based on that selection (Figure 1.25).

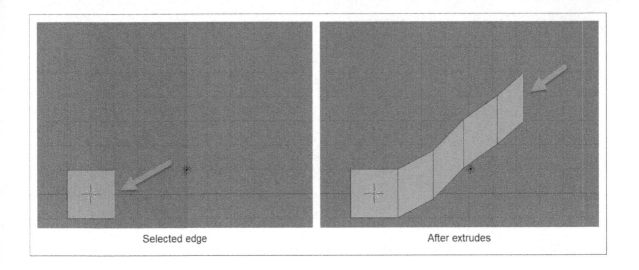

Figure 1.25 - *Extruding shapes*

After you trigger an extrude, it is possible to use numeric input to have better control and precision:

1. Select an edge of vertices

2. Press the E key

3. Press the Y key

4. Type 1

5. Press RETURN to confirm

That small sequence of steps will create a precise extrusion with 1 unit on the Y-axis. If you don't want to use precision, it is also possible to make an extrude with a "free" shape by pressing the E key and moving the mouse cursor anywhere you want. With a left-click, you will confirm the extrude location.

In chapter 3, we will learn more about how you can use the extrude to create 2D walls.

1.5 Precision drawing and units

Right after you trigger an extrusion in Blender, it will be possible to use numeric input to have full control over the length of your extrude. The values you type will use a unit called "Blender Units", which is an abstract value used only in Blender. However, you can choose to use real-world units for your projects.

To change the units Blender uses for transformation, you will have to open the Scene Properties Tab at the Properties Editor (Figure 1.26).

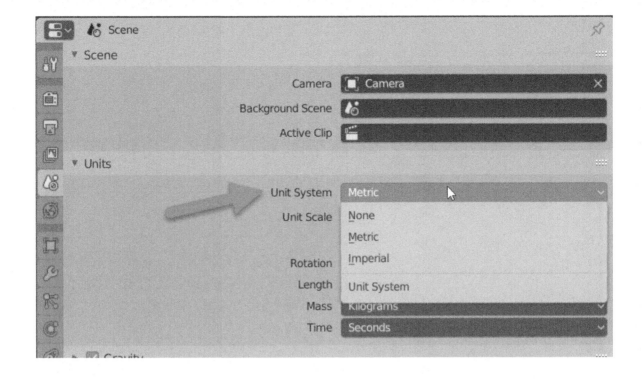

Figure 1.26 - Units options

There you will be able to choose either the Metric System or the Imperial System. Choosing those systems will make Blender display lengths using options from those particular systems (Figure 1.27).

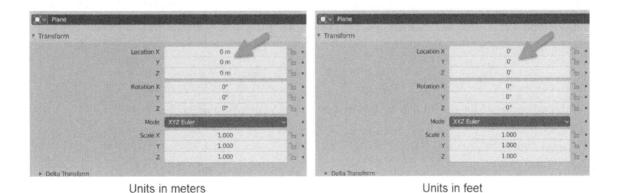

Units in meters   Units in feet

Figure 1.27 - Units for modeling

For instance, you will be able to type values for transformations like:

- 1m

- 50cm

- 1ft or 1'

- 1in or 1"

If you want to model and display units in Blender using the Imperial System, you should also enable an option from the Units settings called "Separate Units" (Figure 1.28).

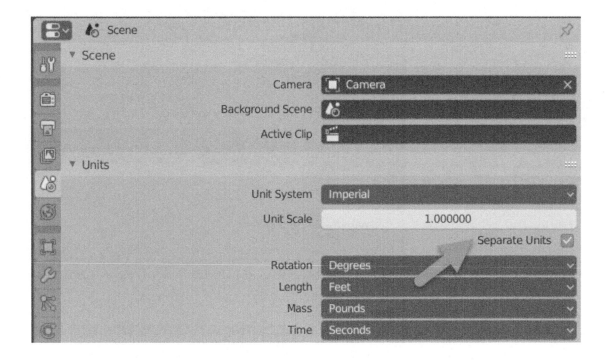

Figure 1.28 - Separate Units

With that option enabled, you will be able to type values with mixed units like:

- 1ft5in

- 2'1"

To type those values for a transformation, you can enable a mode for numeric input in Blender called advance mode. Press the = key to allow that method. For instance, you can create an extrude using that method by:

1. Selecting vertices or edges of an object in Edit Mode

2. Press the E key

3. Press the X key to limit the extrude to the X-axis

4. Press the = key

5. Type 1ft3in

6. Press RETURN to confirm

The = key will enable you to use expressions for transformations. You can view the values used for numeric transformations at the top left corner of your 3D Viewport (Figure 1.29).

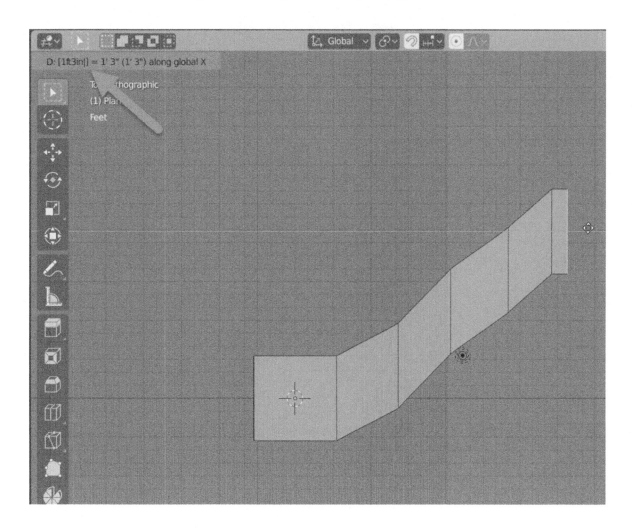

Figure 1.29 - *Numeric transformations*

You can always cancel a transformation in Blender using the ESC key. However, if you plan to cancel an extrude, you should also press the CTRL+Z keys or use the **Edit → Undo** menu to remove the element created by the extruding.

1.5.1 Precision modeling options

What if you have to measure the length of an object in Blender? Some options will allow you to quickly measure the distance between two points or display the length of an edge. Using the Overlays options in Edit Mode, you can enable the display lengths for any selected edges (Figure 1.30).

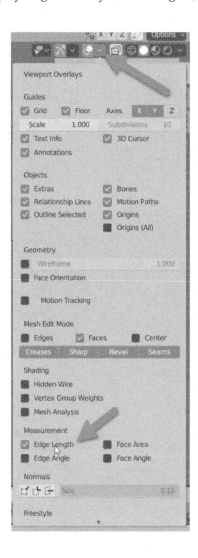

Figure 1.30 - *Overlays options*

Select any edge from the drawing to view the respective length (Figure 1.31).

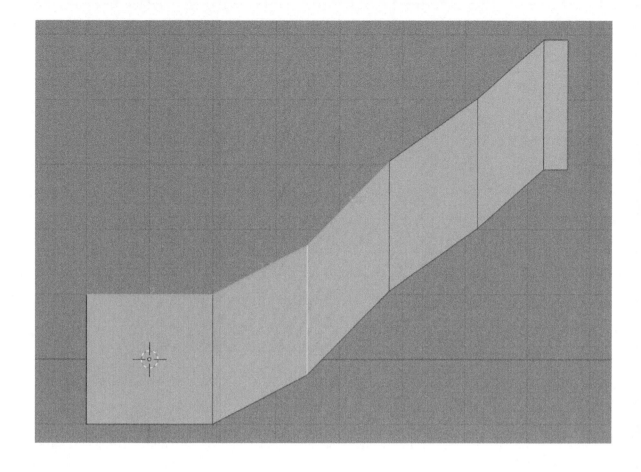

Figure 1.31 - *Edge length*

You can also use the measure option from the Toolbar (Figure 1.32).

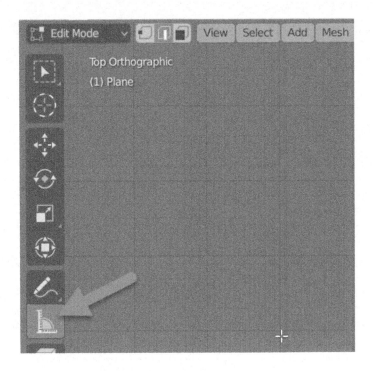

Figure 1.32 - Measure option

The measure option will create a ruler that displays the length between the two points you mark from the 3D object. You have to click and drag to create the ruler. Hold the CTRL key while you drag the mouse to snap and capture points from the 3D object (Figure 1.33).

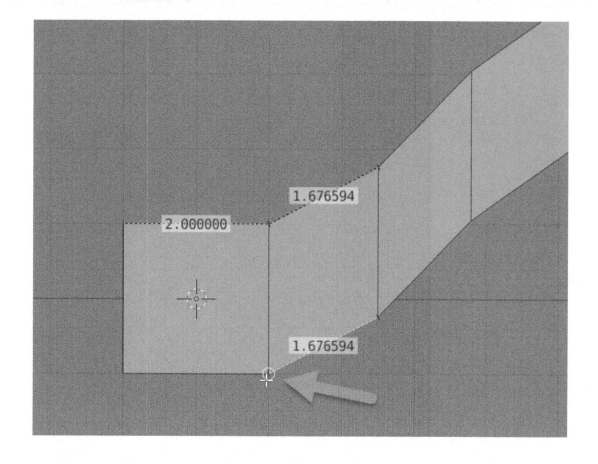

Figure 1.33 - *Ruler from measure tool*

One of the advantages of using the Measure tool is that it doesn't depend on the existence of an edge to show you a length. You can later delete the ruler by selecting it and pressing the DELETE key.

1.6 Shading modes for 2D drawing

The shading modes in Blender will become a critical part of your workflow regarding technical drawing, because it will allow you to have a better understanding of the overall shape of your 3D objects. You will always start Blender in a mode called "Shaded" and you can easily change those modes using the selector available in the 3D Viewport header (Figure 1.34).

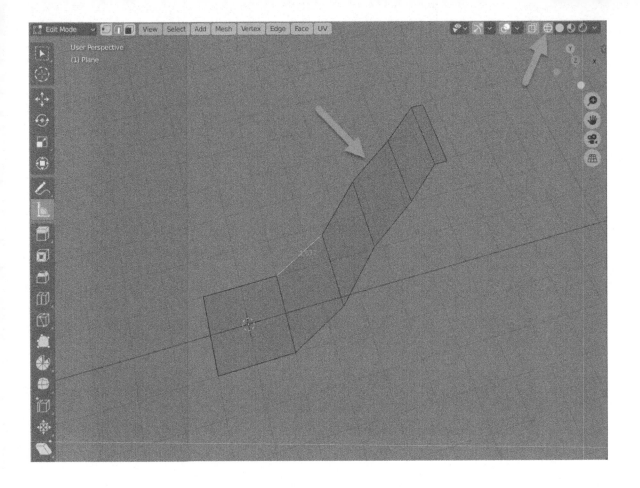

Figure 1.34 - Shading mode selector

For technical drawing you will find that working in a mode called Wireframe will give you the best results regarding visualization and editing. To activate Wireframe mode, you can use the first button from the selector, or you can also use the Z key to swap between each mode (Figure 1.35) quickly.

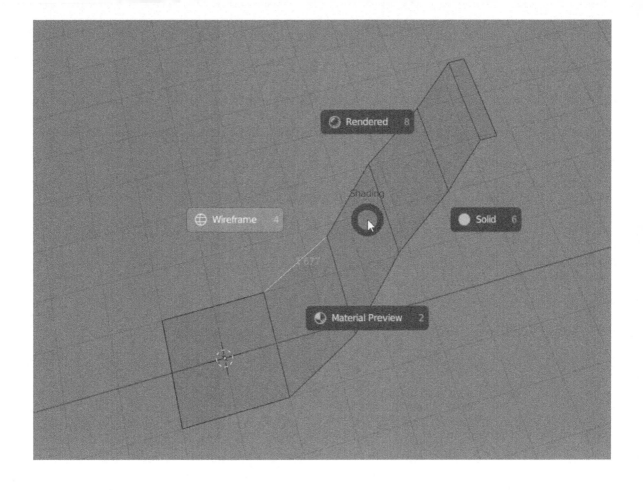

Figure 1.35 - Shading mode with the Z key

Since we will not work with realistic renders when producing technical drawing you will hardly need to use the last two options, which are:

- Material Preview

- Rendered

In the next chapters, you will start to work with a rendering technique that will add strokes to objects and doesn't appear at the 3D Viewport previews.

What is next?

If you have previous experiences with technical drawing production, you will find that Blender is a very different tool from CAD software. The interface and workflows necessary to create 2D drawings have a unique set of options and tools, which may give you the false impression that you are not using the right tool to produce technical drawings.

However, after a few projects and with some more practice, you will start to find solutions to common drawing problems and become more familiar with the tools and interface. The secret to improving your productivity is practice.

With that in mind, you should start trying to create as many 2D drawings using a combination of extruding and numeric inputs. That will help you solidify the knowledge necessary to begin making any drawing in Blender.

In Chapter 3, we will start to produce a floor plan entirely in Blender with the use of extruding and a lot more tools and options.

Chapter 2 - Rendering lines for technical drawing

As a starting point to create technical drawings with Blender, we must understand how it can render lines generated from 3D Objects. The trick to create those lines is using a tool called FreeStyle. It can take 3D objects and add a stroke on each object border.

The following chapter will introduce FreeStyle in Blender with a full description of why you should use Cycles for render and also filter only the parts you need for rendering.

Here is a list of what you will learn:

- How to render lines for technical drawing

- Preparing a project for rendering

- How display only lines for rendering

- Preparing the background for rendering

- Working with Collections

- Selecting edges for rendering

2.1 How to render lines for technical drawing?

To work with technical drawings in Blender, we must learn how to prepare the render settings to create only lines from 3D objects, which will later become technical drawings. By default, if you try to render anything in Blender, you won't see any border or lines surrounding objects.

As part of Blender, we have an interesting render effect called FreeStyle that will help us adding those lines to objects. With the use of FreeStyle, we can add an outline to 3D models in Blender and perform several additional effects. You can set the thickness of those borders and also choose one specific edge to render.

You will find the FreeStyle option available at the Render Properties tab (Figure 2.1).

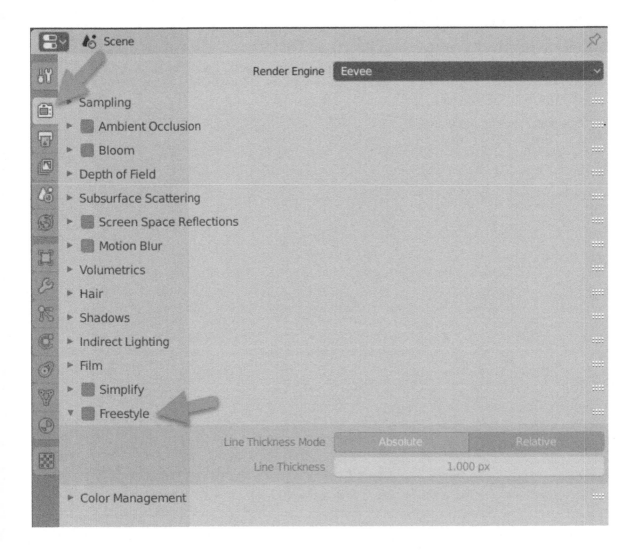

Figure 2.1 - *FreeStyle option*

After enabling that option in your render, it will be possible to add an outline to any 3D Model in your scene.

Before we start rendering some objects using FreeStyle options, it is important to set the differences when choosing either Eevee or Cycles in Blender. You will find two options for rendering in Blender:

– Cycles

– Eevee

With Cycles, you have a traditional render engine that uses a Path Tracing algorithm to create realistic and accurate renders. It is a powerful option to create renders that need cutting-edge realism. It will take a while to process each image, but the results are impressive.

A more recent option is Eevee that can deliver images with exceptional quality in realtime. When comparing with Cycles, you will get images that won't look as good with Eevee but with a fraction of the render time.

For technical drawing rendering, it doesn't make much difference in render quality of you choose either one of them because we will only get a collection of strokes and lines in our final render.

However, due to the nature of how both renderers work, you will find unique options regarding render settings when selecting Cycles or Eevee. Regarding technical drawing, you will find that one critical set of options is not available for Eevee.

Later in the settings, we will use a panel from the View Layer Properties called Filter. In Figure 2.2, you can see the options available for Cycles.

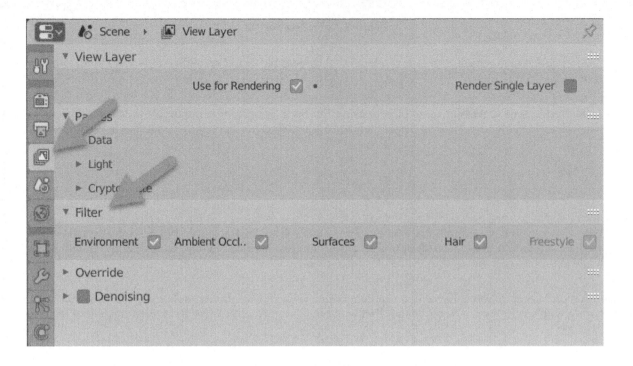

Figure 2.2 - *Cycles Filter options for rendering*

How does the Filter options look like in Eevee? It doesn't exist in Eevee. For that reason, you will only be able to render projects with all surfaces from the scene.

The main purpose of the Filter settings in Cycles is to disable the rendering of all surfaces from 3D Objects. For technical drawing, it will help to create a "clean" visualization of your project with no visible 3D surfaces. You can see the results of a render that uses filtering in Cycles and another with Eevee in Figure 2.3.

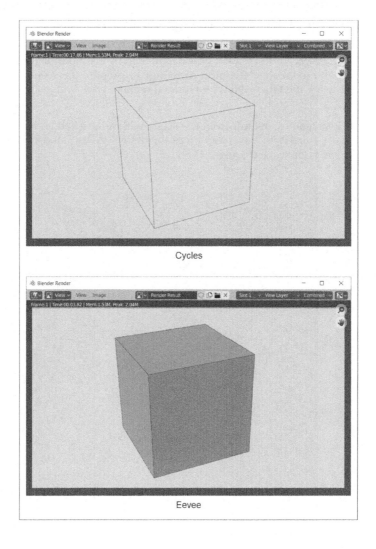

Figure 2.3 - Comparing filtering results

Notice how the image from Eevee will still display strokes for 3D Objects and also surfaces. The render using Cycles that has uses filtering can display only the lines.

For that reason, you should use only Cycles for rendering technical drawings. That will give you an option to filter 3D surfaces from objects and get only the outline from 3D models. The render times for both Cycles and Eevee will be similar because what matters for technical drawing is the stroke rendering.

Regardless of the renderer used, you will get the same processing time to generate strokes.

2.2 Preparing a project for rendering with FreeStyle

We can start working with FreeStyle to create a quick render from a simple object like a plane that later could become a starting point to create a technical drawing. To prepare the scene for rendering, you can start a new file in Blender using the **File → New → General** menu.

Select the cube that is available by default from the scene with a left-click and press either DELETE or the X key. It will remove the cube from the scene. Press the SHIFT+A keys and choose **Mesh → Plane**. It will create a new 3D plane in your scene (Figure 2.4).

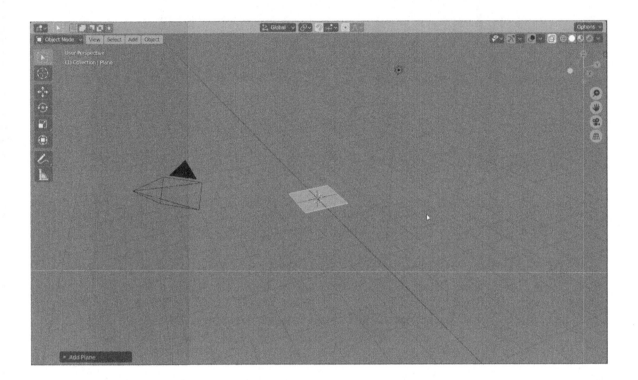

Figure 2.4 - New 3D Plane

The next step is to prepare the camera to view our scene from the top. Assuming you have only one camera in the scene, we can align it in the top position:

1. Press the Numpad 7 or use the **View → Viewport → Top** menu. The shortcut will change your view to the top.

2. To align the camera, you can press the CTRL+ALT+Numpad 0 keys. You can also use the **View → Align View → Align Active Camera to View** menu.

3. Select the camera border and open the Object Data Properties tab.

4. From the Type selector, you can change the camera from Perspective to Orthographic.

5. Use the Orthographic Scale to adjust the zoom and the G key to move your camera.

After performing all those steps, you should have an orthographic camera viewing the scene from the top (Figure 2.5).

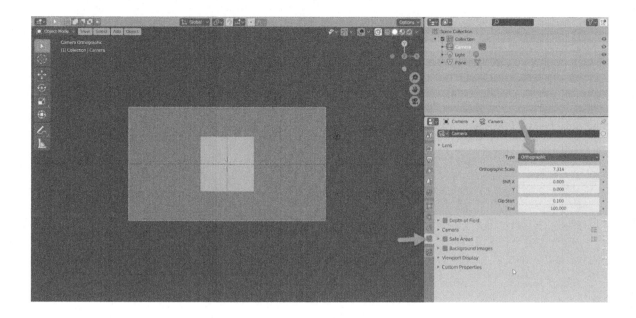

Figure 2.5 - Camera from the top

For technical drawing rendering where you must create 2D renders, you will use those same steps to prepare the scene. Before we start rendering the scene, we have to make two last adjustments. The first one is to pick a color for the background of our scene.

Go to the World Properties tab and set the Surface Color to white (Figure 2.6).

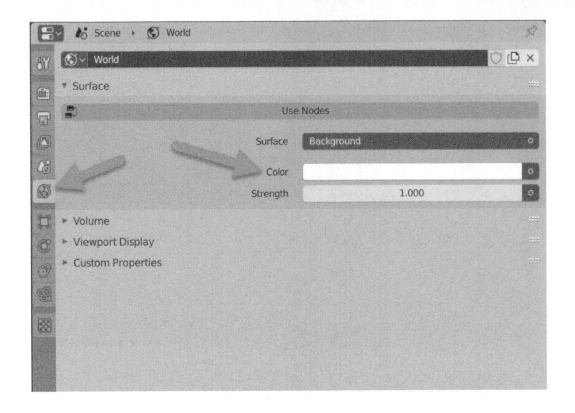

Figure 2.6 - *Background color*

And finally, you should select Cycles as your renderer in the Render Properties settings (Figure 2.7).

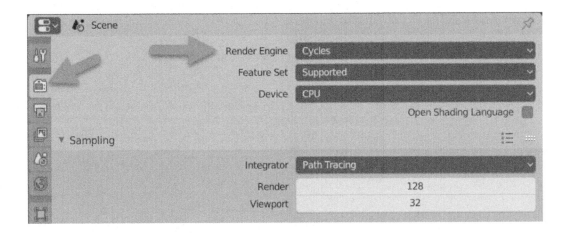

Figure 2.7 - *Cycles as renderer*

Later we can make additional adjustments to fine-tune our render and technical drawing.

Before the first render, you can also adjust the output size of your image at the Output Properties tab. The tab is below your render options and has right at the top of a field called Dimensions. By default, Blender will start rendering images with a 1920 x 1080 px resolution. You can change those values in that tab.

Making changes to the render size will also alter the camera aspect ration. For instance, if you change the render dimensions to a squared size like 2048 x 2048 px will also change the aspect of your camera.

For now, you can press the F12 key in your keyboard to start rendering. You will see the plane object appearing in the output window (Figure 2.8).

Figure 2.8 - Plane object

You can save the render results in that window using the Image menu. Choose "Save As…" to save your image as a PNG file. You will find the options to choose a format for your images on the right side of the "Blender File View" window. The next step is to enable FreeStyle rendering for our project.

Tip: You can quickly reduce your render output size with the scale options. For instance, using a factor of 50% will cut in half the output size. Open the Output Properties tab, which is below your render settings and look for the "%" field at the top of that panel.

Go to the Render Properties tab and look for the FreeStyle option. You can enable the FreeStyle in that panel (Figure 2.9).

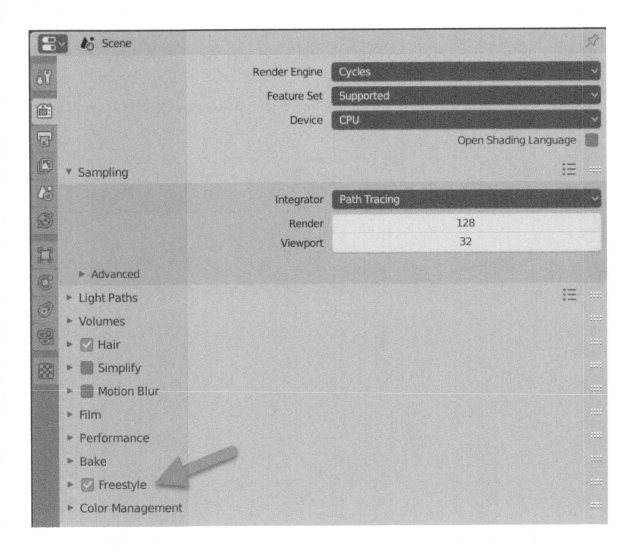

Figure 2.9 - *FreeStyle in Render*

Once you enable the FreeStyle option, press the F12 key again to start a new render. You will notice that our plane object now has an outline in all edges (Figure 2.10).

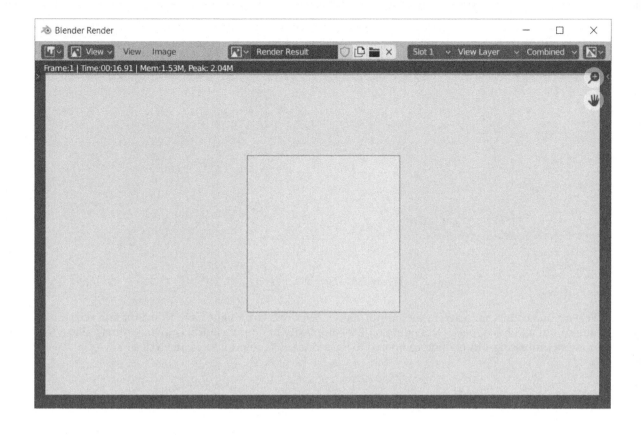

Figure 2.10 - *Plane with outline*

You can later change the settings for FreeStyle to control aspects of the stokes like thickness and alignment. Enabling FreeStyle is the easiest step in the process. Since we are using an orthographic camera viewing the scene from the top, instead of a 3D plane, we will get a 2D square as the render.

2.2.1 Generating strokes for technical drawing

From a rendering point of view, you will see that creating the strokes for a 2D drawing in Blender is much faster than a traditional render. After you have the scene processed, you will see a message at the top of your output window showing that FreeStyle is creating the lines (Figure 2.11).

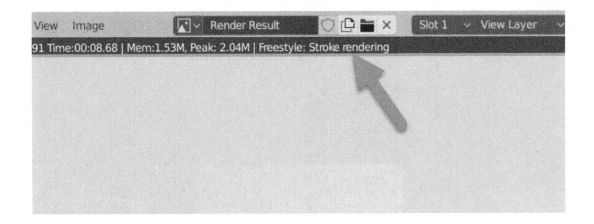

Figure 2.11 - *Stroke processing*

When you see that message in the output render window, you might have to wait a few seconds or minutes until all lines appear. Depending on the complexity of your technical drawing, it may take a few minutes of processing, but nothing compared to the render of an interior scene in Cycles.

2.3 Filtering only lines for rendering

It is now time to use the Filter option from the View Layer Properties tab. If you have Cycles selected as the primary renderer, you will see a panel inside the View Layer Properties called Filter. There you can disable certain parts of your render.

For instance, you can disable the "Surfaces" option to hide all 3D surfaces from the render (Figure 2.12).

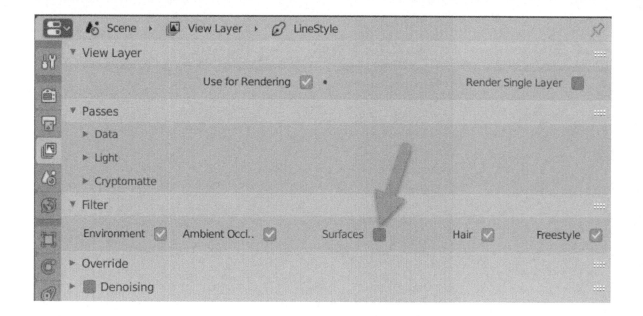

Figure 2.12 - *Disable Surfaces*

By disabling the Surfaces and pressing F12 to start a new render, you will notice that your 3D plane will now only display the strokes and no surface (Figure 2.13).

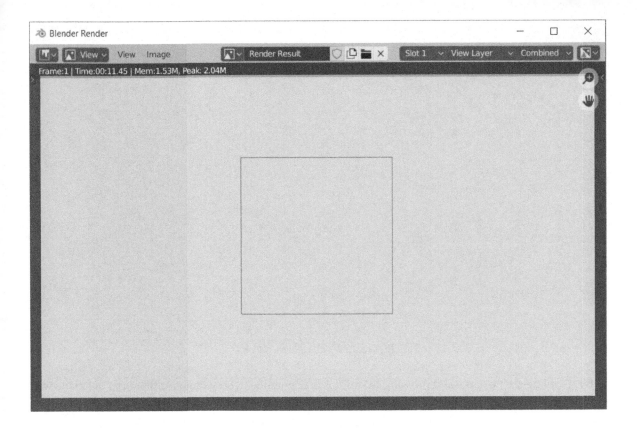

Figure 2.13 - Object render with no surfaces

That is how we will create technical drawings displaying only the lines generated by FreeStyle. To create the lines, we need 3D objects in your scene because FreeStyle can only create strokes for existing models. But, in a project where you want to see strokes and no additional objects, the Filter option is incredibly important.

2.4 Preparing the background for rendering

If you follow the steps described in section 2.2 (Preparing a project for rendering with FreeStyle), you will have a square-shaped object in a white background. However, if you take a close look at the background color, you will notice it is not white.

By using the World Properties alone and choosing white color for the Surface settings, you will get a light grey color instead of white. The main reason for this is because Cycles uses a color profile called "filmic" by default, which will change the way it processes colors.

It is an incredible profile for rendering realistic images and interiors for architecture, but won't help us working in technical drawing rendering. To get a plain white background for our technical drawings, we have to make a few changes in the color management options.

Go to the Render Properties tab and locate the Color Management options (Figure 2.14).

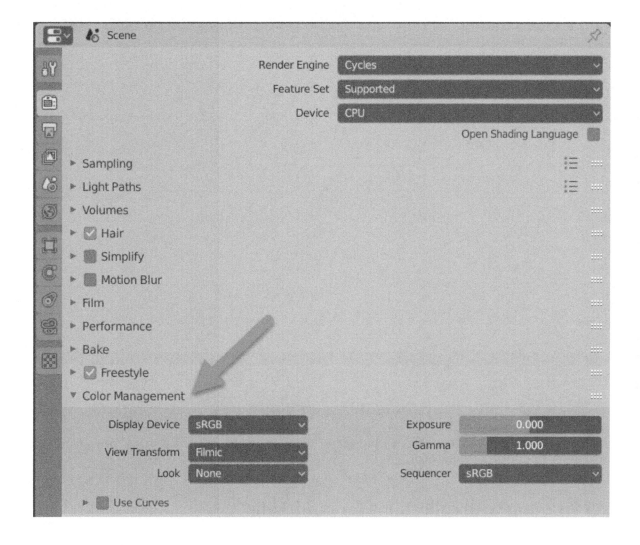

Figure 2.14 - *Color Management*

There you will have to make changes to two settings:

- **View Transform**: Change from filmic to Standard
- **Look**: Change from None to Base Contrast

If you choose the options described for the two fields in the Color Management, you will get a plain white background when rendering (Figure 2.15).

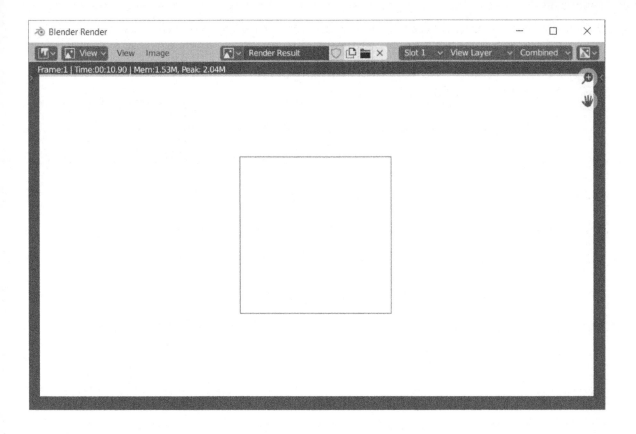

Figure 2.15 - *Plain white background*

For projects where you have to work with realistic rendering with Cycles, you should use the default options for View Transform and Look.

2.5 Working with collections for rendering

At this point, we are rendering a scene that has only a single 3D plane that looks like a square object in the output window. Assuming you want to render all objects from a scene, we could stop making any changes to the FreeStyle settings. But, as you will see later in the book, we often have to create additional elements that should not be in a render.

By default, you will get strokes for all objects in the scene when rendering with FreeStyle. If you have a 3D object in the scene and activate FreeStyle, all objects will receive an outline.

We have several ways to control which objects should appear in a render with an outline using FreeStyle. A simple and effective way to control that is with Collections.

2.5.1 Using Collections to filter objects

The Collections in Blender gives you a lot of control over object visibility and scene organization. You will see a list with all Collections available at the scene in your Outliner Editor (Figure 2.16).

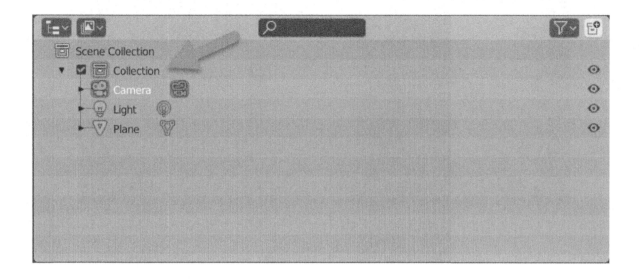

Figure 2.16 - *Collections*

A scene in Blender will always start with a Scene Collection that will hold all additional Collections in the project. You will have at least one Collection with all objects in the project.

To show how you can use Collections to organize and control stroke generation, we can take the same scene used until this point in the chapter. Select the 3D plane and press the SHIFT+D keys. That will duplicate the object.

Press the X key and move the new plane object to the left. With a left-click, you can confirm the object position (Figure 2.17).

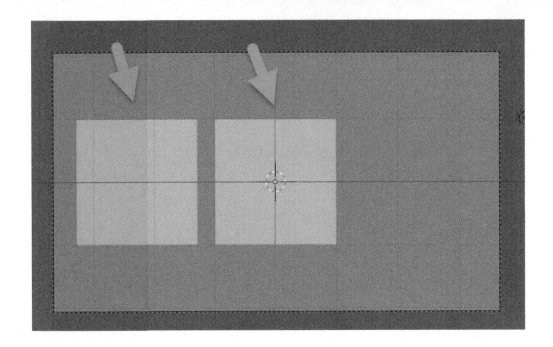

Figure 2.17 - *Two planes*

If you press F12 at this point, you will have two squares in the output window with strokes generated by FreeStyle. What if we only wanted the strokes from the plane on the right?

You can limit the stroke generation in your render using Collections. In the FreeStyle settings, we can set the stroke generation to only a single Collection. To get that working, we have to create a unique Collection for the plane on the right.

Select that object and press the M key in Object Mode. That will make a small menu appear with options related to Collections. Choose the "+ New Collection" (Figure 2.18).

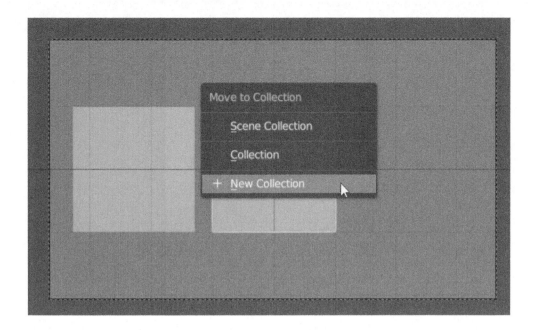

Figure 2.18 - *New Collection*

Assign a name to that Collection that will help identify their purpose. In our case, a name like "Right-Plane" will work.

Tip: *The same M key will also help you manage and move objects between existing Collections. It is also possible to click and drag objects between Collections at the Outliner Editor.*

If you look at the Outliner Editor, a new Collection is available there and has our plane object (Figure 2.19).

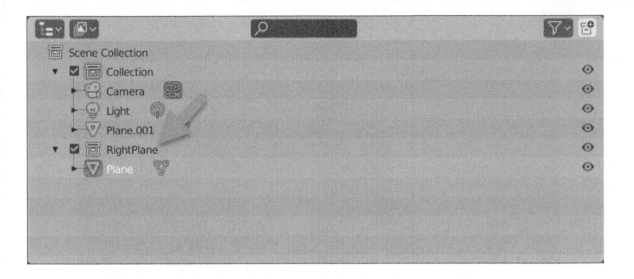

Figure 2.19 - Collection with plane

You can also create new Collections straight from the Outliner Editor using a right-click. After creating the Collection, it is only a matter of clicking and dragging objects to the Collection you want to use.

2.5.2 Filtering the render by Collection

With a Collection that all the objects we want to use for rendering with FreeStyle, it is time to make the adjustments to the render output. At the View Layer Properties you will find two panels with lots of options for FreeStyle:

– FreeStyle Line Set

– FreeStyle Line Style

They will help us choosing how the strokes from FreeStyle will appear in the final render (Figure 2.20).

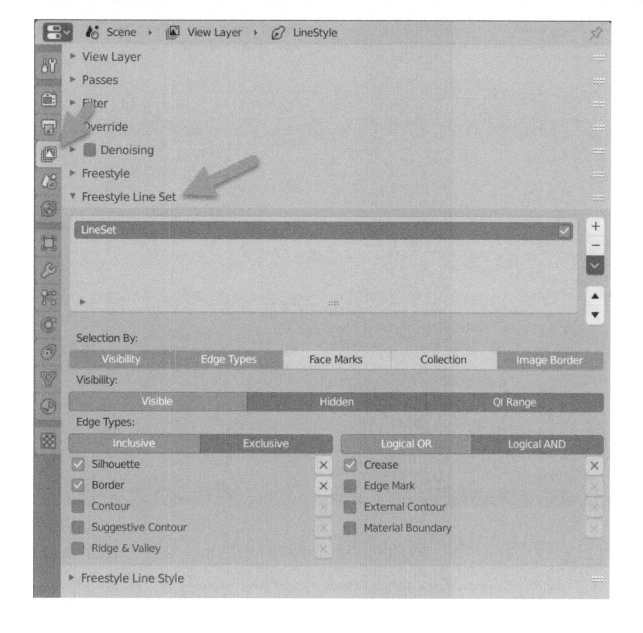

Figure 2.20 - *FreeStyle Options*

One of the most basic options in the Line Set is the selection of what properties of an object we can use to generate strokes. At the "Select By" options, you will see three buttons enabled by default:

- Visibility

- Edge Types

- Image Border

Those will control what types of objects can generate strokes in a render. Among the options, you will see a button for Collections. Press that button, and a new field appears at the bottom (Figure 2.21).

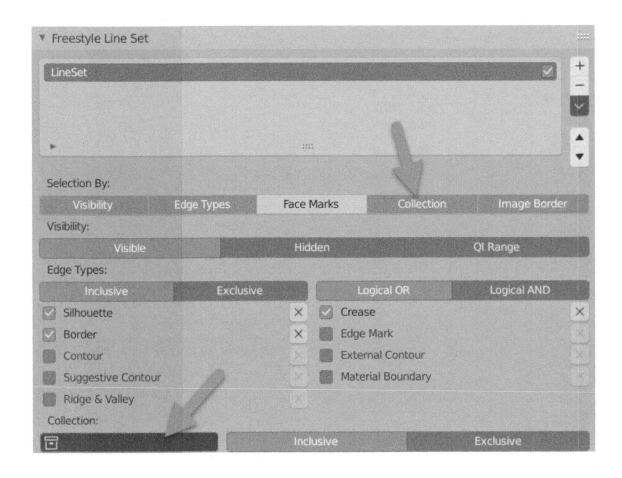

Figure 2.21 - Collections option

In the new field, you can choose a single Collection that will use all settings from the Line Set. If you add the "RightPlane" Collection to the selector, you will make it use only the objects at that particular Collection for rendering.

After pressing F12 to render, you will no longer see a border for the plane on the left side (Figure 2.22).

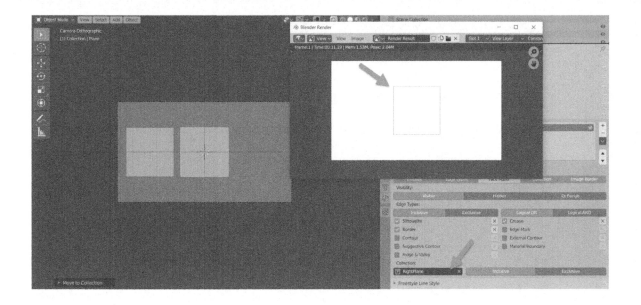

Figure 2.22 - Rendering only one Collection

Using that option will make FreeStyle add a stroke to all objects inside the "RightPlane" Collection. Next to the Collection selector, you can see two additional buttons:

– Inclusive

– Exclusive

The default option is Inclusive, which will only render the contents of a single Collection. By choosing the Exclusive, you will render all Collections but the one selected.

2.6 Selecting edges from 3D models to render

The possibility to select what you want to render and also add strokes with FreeStyle is essential for technical drawing, but sometimes you need an extra level of control. What if you only wanted to render two edges from a plane? Besides using Collections to filter what we won't use in a render, it is also possible to select specific edges from objects.

By default, you will see strokes from all edges from 3D models in FreeStyle. But, if you select any object and go to Edit Mode, we can use something called FreeStyle Edge to have a higher level of control. For instance, we can take the plane object used across this chapter and only render the two edges shown in Figure 2.23.

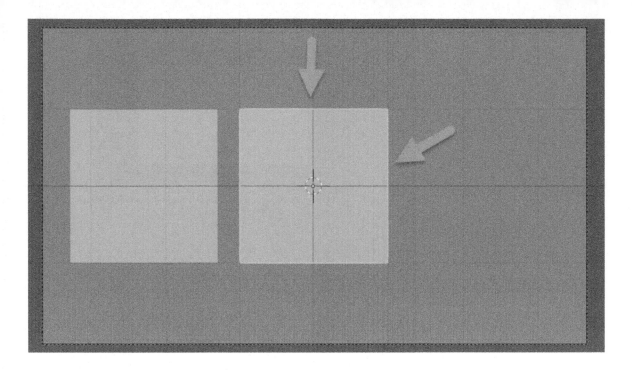

Figure 2.23 - Edges to render

The first step to set up only those two edges to render is selecting the object and change the work mode to Edit. You can quickly do that by pressing the TAB key. Once in Edit Mode, you must set the selection mode to Edge (Figure 2.24).

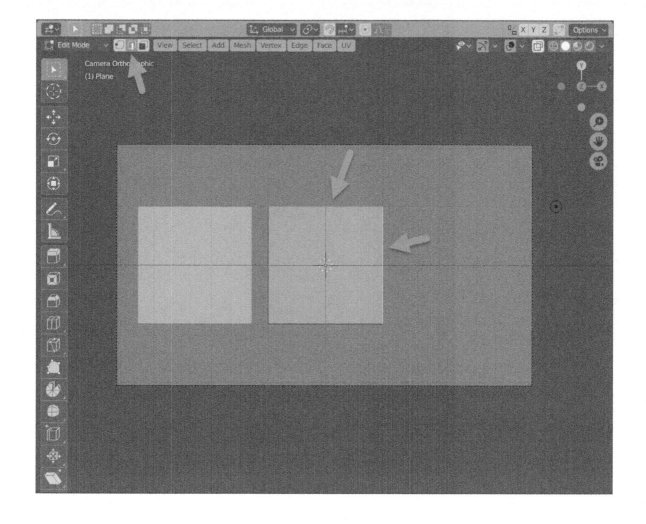

Figure 2.24 - Selection mode to edge

Using that mode will make the context menu from Blender to display options related to edges. To make FreeStyle add strokes to only a few selected edges, we have to select them first. You can click at the first edge and hold the SHIFT click while clicking on more edges.

Select as many edges you want to use for rendering strokes. Once you have all the edges selected, press the right mouse button. It will open the context menu (Figure 2.25).

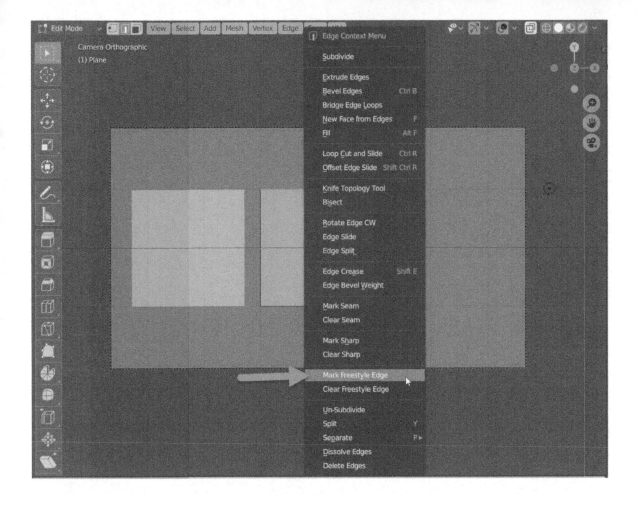

Figure 2.25 - Edge context menu

There you will find two options for FreeStyle:

– Mark FreeStyle Edge

– Clear FreeStyle Edge

With the "Mark FreeStyle Edge" you can highlight any selected edges for rendering with FreeStyle. It would be like flagging those edges for later use. The Clear FreeStyle Edge removes that marking. You will notice that once an edge has that mark, it will display a different color (Figure 2.26).

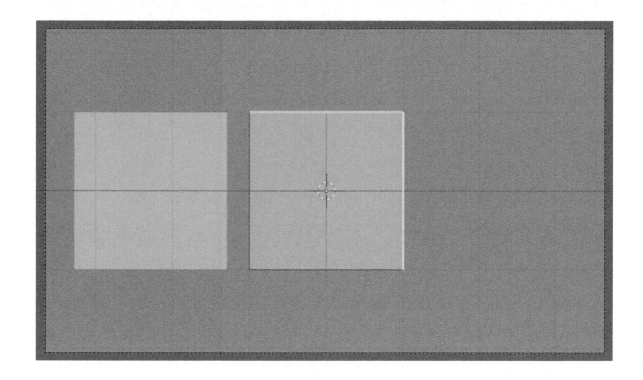

Figure 2.26 - *FreeStyle Edge*

After adding the mark to the edges, we can go back to the View Layer Properties and the FreeStyle settings. There you will find the Line Set options where we can use the marks. Notice that in the "Edge Types" field, you have all the types of edges FreeStyle will use to add strokes (Figure 2.27).

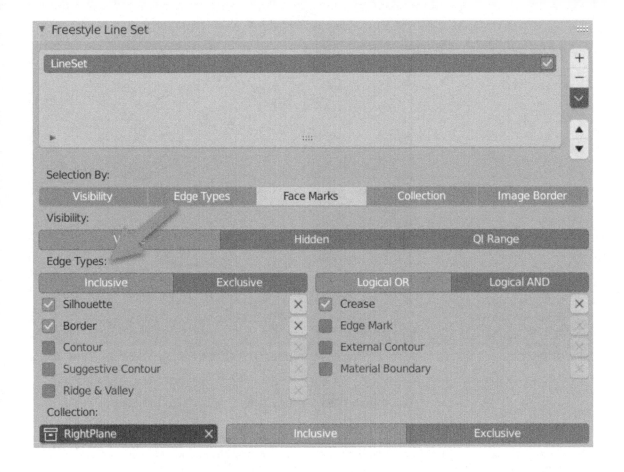

Figure 2.27 - Edge Types

Since we want full control over the edges used for rendering, you can disable all options and leave only "Edge Mark" as the edge selected for rendering. It will make FreeStyle add strokes to the edges having a mark only.

If you press the F12 key now, you will only see the strokes showing up at the edges that have a mark (Figure 2.28).

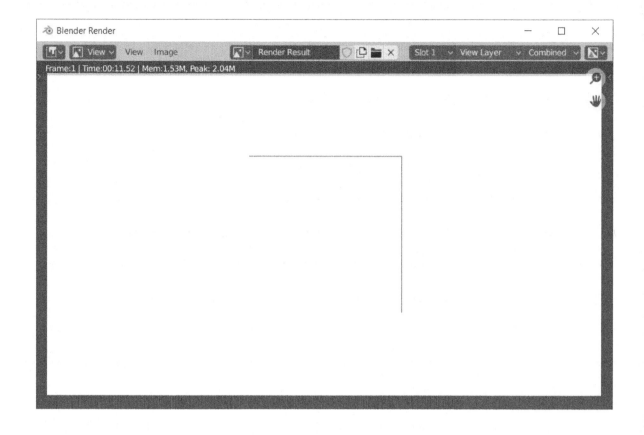

Figure 2.28 - Strokes for edges with marks

That is the best way to have full control over which edges you will have in a render receiving stokes from FreeStyle. If you use that alongside Collections for Line Sets, you have a powerful and flexible way to select parts of a model that should receive strokes.

It will become incredibly useful to use those marks for edges when we must create certain symbols for technical drawing. For instance, you can develop arcs for doors by selecting only the curved part of a 3D mesh.

Tip: *In Edit Mode, you will also find options to add and remove FreeStyle Marks from the Edge menu. The menu is available even if you don't have your selection mode set for edges.*

What is next?

The creation of technical drawing in Blender uses as a base the FreeStyle render options, and after you start to use them to add strokes to 3D shapes, it will become easy to make stylized images. In our examples, we added the strokes to simple objects like a flat 2D plane, but you can use any 3D object to add an outline.

You can use the settings from FreeStyle to start making renders using unique visuals with thickness, shapes, and lines to your projects.

An option that has a great impact on productivity for technical drawing is the use of Collections, which will help us control how each line renders. If you don't have the habit of getting your 3D objects in unique collections, it is a great way to start organizing them using such a feature.

Always try to use the M key to place your objects in a unique Collection.

Chapter 3 - Drawing in 2D using Blender (Floor plan)

After you started with Blender and learned how to make 2D renderings with the FreeStyle settings, it is time to put that knowledge to create a technical drawing. In this chapter, we will start the design process of a floor plan. The objective is to create a prepare a floor plan design for print or display in a monitor.

You will create the walls, doors, windows, and add dimension lines. At the beginning of the design process, we will focus on the walls creation and the creation of placeholders for doors and windows.

Here is a list of what you will learn:

- Drawing a floor plan

- Creating the walls

- Making curved walls

- Working with doors and windows

- Drawing the stairs

- Creating the external area

- Preparing the floor plan for rendering

3.1 Drawing a floor plan

After looking at how you can create a render with FreeStyle in Blender that will allow us to produce technical drawings, it is time to start working at an actual drawing. In Blender, you will find a lot of options and tools to create 3D models. Those tools will also help us creating full-featured technical drawings for multiple purposes.

It could be the representation of an architectural, mechanical, or industrial design drawing. Regardless of the destination and use of those drawings, you will apply similar concepts during creation.

As a way to demonstrate how you can draw a technical drawing, we will start making a floor plan in this chapter, which will receive all the necessary symbols, annotations, and features of a traditional technical drawing.

The final drawing you will create in the last chapters of the book will look like Figure 3.1 shows.

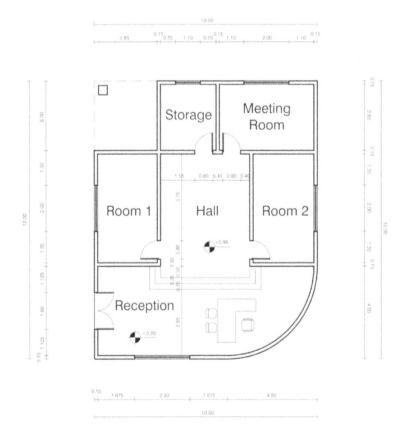

Figure 3.1 - Floor plan in Blender

For this chapter, we will start the process with the drawing stage, where the architectural elements for the floor plan will be the focus. Using Blender tools for 3D modeling, it will be possible to draw:

- Walls

- Doors

- Windows

- Projections

At the end of this chapter, you will have a floor plan that will be ready to receive settings and adjustments to render a technical drawing. The final result for this chapter will look like Figure 3.2 shows.

Figure 3.2 - *Floor plan from chapter*

As you can see from Figure 3.2, the floor plan is a 3D model that we create in Blender using tools related to modeling. There is no special mode or option for 2D drawings related to a technical drawing.

An important aspect of the floor plan drawing is the use of dimensions to create such drawings. Usually, when you are designing a floor plan, you will start working with a few ideas about lengths and dimensions, but you don't have a finished design yet. For that reason, a technical drawing will not use a reference image for drawing.

Since you are in the design and concept stage for the project, you will have to evaluate and decide each dimension as you will draw the walls and architectural elements.

However, you can start working with at least two basic dimensions for the building we will draw:

- **Maximum width**: 12
- **Maximum height**: 10

Those will be the limits for the building concerning the site. Inside those limits, we can design our walls in any way we like.

3.2 Creating the walls

Now that we have some basic information regarding the shape and look of our floor plan, it is time to start "drawing" the walls. Is it possible to draw in 2D in Blender? From a technical drawing point of view, we cant "draw" in 2D using precision.

To create a floor plan or any other technical drawing, we will use a procedure that will transform a 3D model in a flat 2D drawing. Using that technique will allow you to use all precision tools from Blender to create an accurate drawing, and have a flat design rendered only with lines at the end.

If you remember the 3D Plane we used in chapter 2 that ended up as a square after rendering, we will use a similar approach with the floor plan. Since the floor plan will use flat design, we can start with a 3D Plane.

Info: There is no need to make adjustments to the camera settings at this moment because our focus will be solely on the modeling tasks.

3.2.1 Starting the drawing of a floor plan

Start a new project file in Blender using the **File** → **New** menu and choose General. Select the Cube from the startup file and delete it. Press the SHIFT+A keys and create a Plane from the Mesh group.

A plane in Blender will always start with a size of two Blender units for each side. Since we are working with a technical drawing, you will want to have full control over scales and dimensions. You can use the settings from Scene Properties to choose either the Metric or Imperial systems for modeling.

For this example, I will use the Blender Units system, but you can adapt the procedure to use Meters or Feet and Inches. In chapter 1, we explained how to use and setup both systems.

After creating the 3D plane, you will see it like Figure 3.3 shows. Since the walls will have a 0.15 thickness for this drawing, we must use a scale transformation to the object.

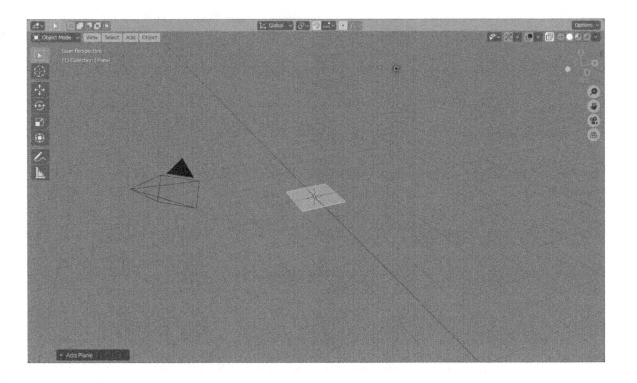

Figure 3.3 - Stating plane

With the plane selected:

1. Press the S key to start a scale transformation

2. Type 0.075

3. Press RETURN to confirm

4. Press CTRL+A and choose Scale

That will scale the 3D plane down and make each edge to have 0.15 units in length. The last step with the CTRL+A applies the scale to the plane and removes any scale factor.

From the 3D plane, we can choose any wall intersection to start drawing the floor plan. As an example, we can consider the plane in a location like the bottom left corner (Figure 3.4).

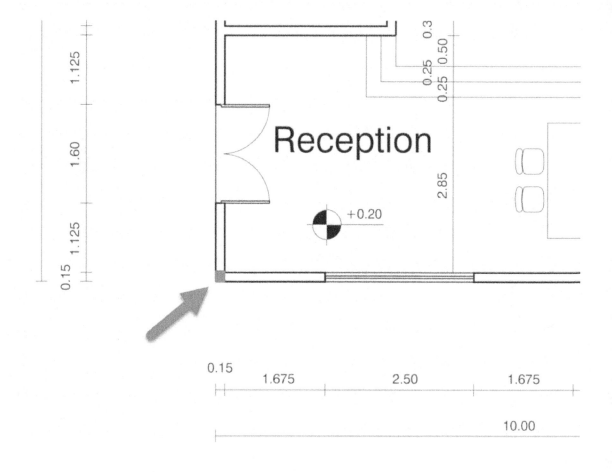

Figure 3.4 - Plane location

The next step now is to create a sequence of planes using the extrude tool in Blender. You can select an edge from the plane and start working on extrudes. In the following sequence, we will create a total of eight extrudes.

You have to make all extrude in the Y-axis and follow a sequence of lengths to create each wall. In Edit Mode, select the top edge of your plane (Figure 3.5).

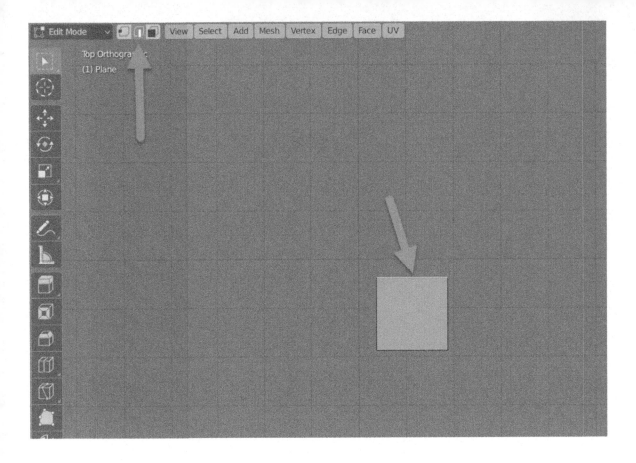

Figure 3.5 - Selected edge

And we can start with the extrudes:

1. Press the E key

2. Press the Y key

3. Type 1.125

4. Press RETURN to confirm

5. Press the E key

6. Press the Y key

7. Type 1.6

8. Press RETURN to confirm

9. Press the E key

10. Press the Y key

11. Type 1.125

12. Press RETURN to confirm

13. Press the E key

14. Press the Y key

15. Type 0.15

16. Press RETURN to confirm

17. Press the E key

18. Press the Y key

19. Type 1.35

20. Press RETURN to confirm

21. Press the E key

22. Press the Y key

23. Type 2

24. Press RETURN to confirm

25. Press the E key

26. Press the Y key

27. Type 1.35

28. Press RETURN to confirm

29. Press the E key

30. Press the Y key

31. Type 0.15

32. Press RETURN to confirm

The long sequence of extrudes will allow you to create all faces required to draw all walls from the left side (Figure 3.6).

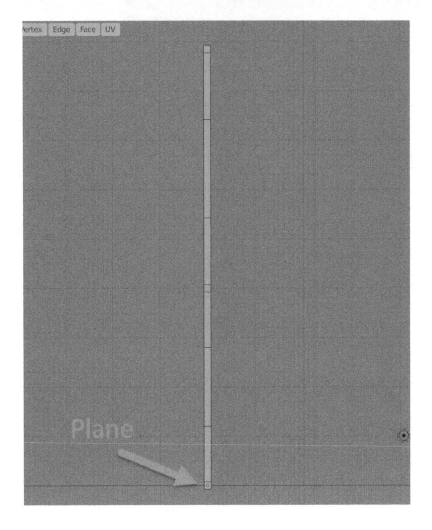

Figure 3.6 - *Walls from left side*

A few things you should consider when drawing using the extrude:

- At any moment you can cancel the extrudes with the ESC key

- If you cancel an extrude, make sure you also press CTRL+Z to undo the edge creation

- Each door and window opening should have a unique plane. Later in the design process, we will remove and edit those planes

As a next step, we can create more walls using existing edges from the model we created. Still, in Edit Mode, select the two small edges on the right side (Figure 3.7).

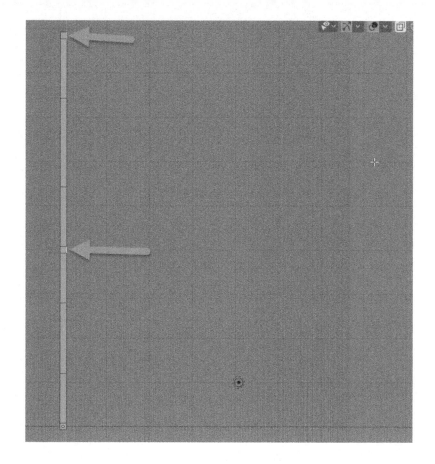

Figure 3.7 - *Edges on the right*

Those two edges will work as a reference for the creation of a segment of walls (Figure 3.8).

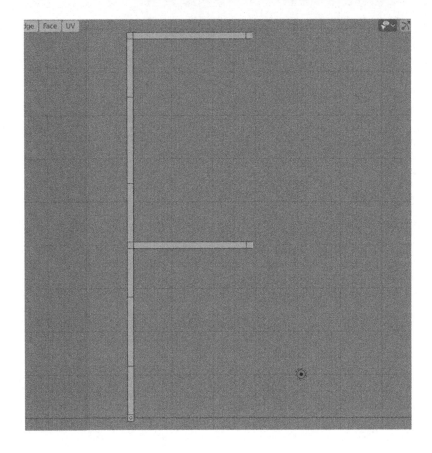

Figure 3.8 - New walls

With the edges selected, we will create two extrudes in the X-axis:

1. Press the E key

2. Press the X key

3. Type 2.7

4. Press RETURN to confirm

5. Press the E key

6. Press the X key

7. Type 0.15

8. Press RETURN to confirm

As a result, we will get two new walls. From the new walls, select the edge shown in Figure 3.9.

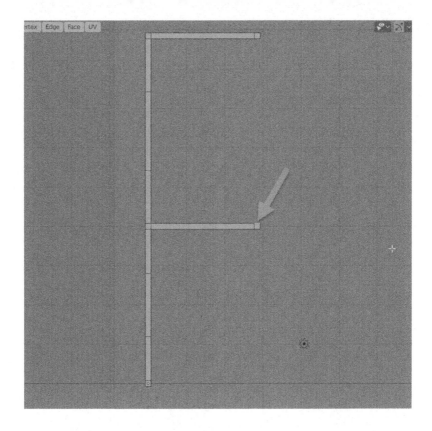

Figure 3.9 - Single edge selected

From that edge we will make a few more extrudes in the Y-axis:

1. Press the E key

2. Press the Y key

3. Type 0.15

4. Press RETURN to confirm

5. Press the E key

6. Press the Y key

7. Type 0.8

8. Press RETURN to confirm

One of the rooms on our floor plan has almost all the walls ready. For the last wall, we could use an extrude, but it would create a double edge at the intersection between two edges. A good way to solve this is with the F key. If you select two edges and press the F key, you will create a plane connecting them.

Select the edges shown in Figure 3.10 and press the F key to connect them with a plane.

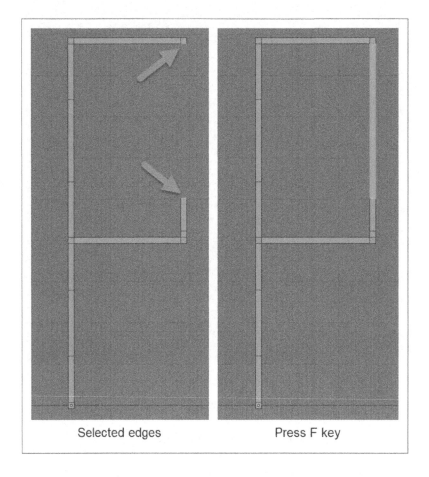

Figure 3.10 - *Selected edges*

The first room has all four walls ready now.

3.2.2 Drawing walls for the top two rooms

With a base for the walls already in place, we can start making the top two rooms. Select the edge shown in Figure 3.11 to start to make two extrudes in the Y-axis.

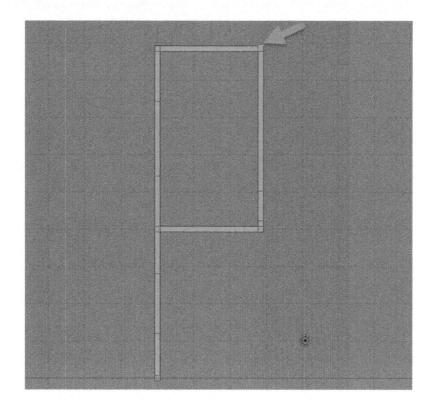

Figure 3.11 - *Top edge selected*

Create two extrudes using the selected edge:

1. Press the E key

2. Press the Y key

3. Type 2.85

4. Press RETURN to confirm

5. Press the E key

6. Press the Y key

7. Type 0.15

8. Press RETURN to confirm

Now, we have to create two sequences of extrudes to build the top and bottom walls for both rooms. First, we will start with the top room selecting the edge on the top right (Figure 3.12).

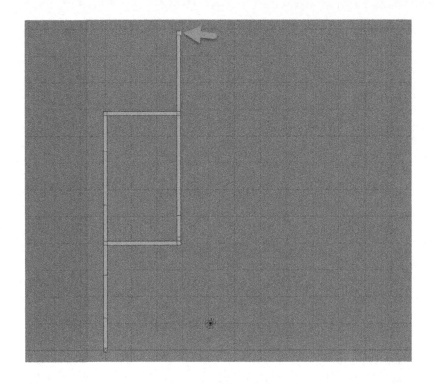

Figure 3.12 - *Top right edge*

Using that selected edge:

1. Press the E key

2. Press the X key

3. Type 0.7

4. Press RETURN to confirm

5. Press the E key

6. Press the X key

7. Type 1.1

8. Press RETURN to confirm

9. Press the E key

10. Press the X key

11. Type 0.7

12. Press RETURN to confirm

13. Press the E key

14. Press the X key

15. Type 0.15

16. Press RETURN to confirm

17. Press the E key

18. Press the X key

19. Type 1.1

20. Press RETURN to confirm

21. Press the E key

22. Press the X key

23. Type 2

24. Press RETURN to confirm

25. Press the E key

26. Press the X key

27. Type 1.1

28. Press RETURN to confirm

29. Press the E key

30. Press the X key

31. Type 0.15

32. Press RETURN to confirm

The result should be a sequential creation of walls for our room (Figure 3.13).

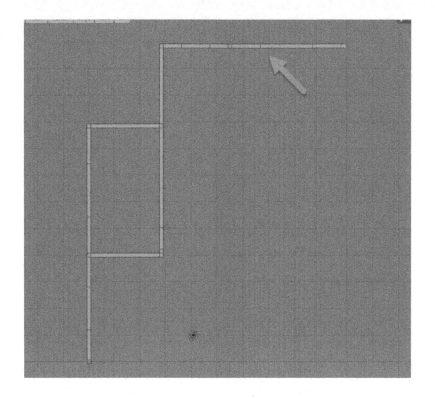

Figure 3.13 - *Top walls for both rooms*

It is now time to create the bottom part of all walls, which will require the selection of an edge shown in Figure 3.14.

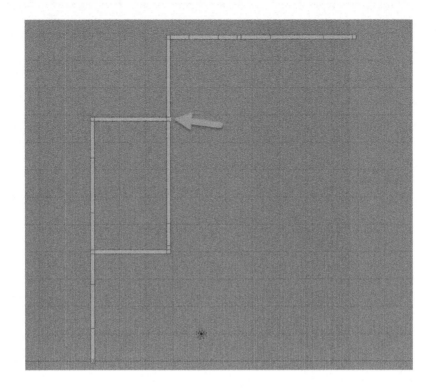

Figure 3.14 - *Bottom edge to start extruding*

With that edge selected:

1. Press the E key

2. Press the X key

3. Type 1.55

4. Press RETURN to confirm

5. Press the E key

6. Press the X key

7. Type 0.8

8. Press RETURN to confirm

9. Press the E key

10. Press the X key

11. Type 0.15

12. Press RETURN to confirm

13. Press the E key

14. Press the X key

15. Type 0.15

16. Press RETURN to confirm

17. Press the E key

18. Press the X key

19. Type 0.15

20. Press RETURN to confirm

21. Press the E key

22. Press the X key

23. Type 0.8

24. Press RETURN to confirm

25. Press the E key

26. Press the X key

27. Type 0.4

28. Press RETURN to confirm

29. Press the E key

30. Press the X key

31. Type 0.15

32. Press RETURN to confirm

33. Press the E key

34. Press the X key

35. Type 2.7

36. Press RETURN to confirm

You should now have two large horizontal walls created from all those extrudes. Using the F key, we can connect the small edges that form each of the vertical walls in both rooms. Select the edges pointed at Figure 3.15 and press the F key.

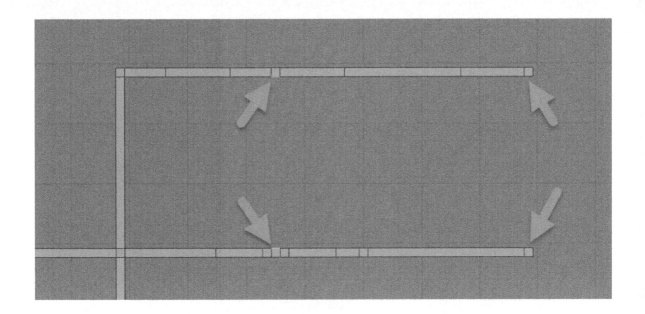

Figure 3.15 - *Edges to connect*

Press the F key when having only two edges selected. Now, all the walls from the top two rooms are ready (Figure 3.16).

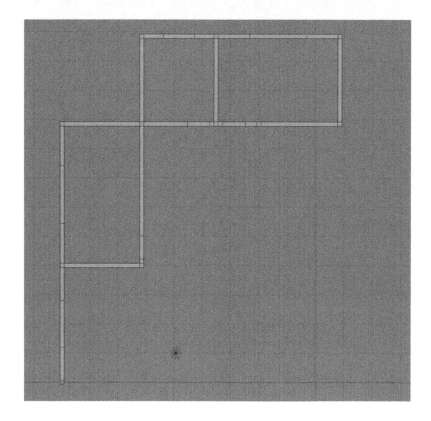

Figure 3.16 - *Walls from top two rooms*

From the sequence of extrudes created until now, you probably realized that it is a repetitive task, and with the lengths in mind, you can quickly create walls for any floor plan design in Blender.

3.2.3 Drawing walls with the snap tool

The next room we will draw is the one on the right side of our floor plan, which has the same dimensions from the same room on the left. Instead of using a long sequence of extrudes with lengths typed from the keyboard, we can use the existing vertices from our room on the left.

You can use a tool in Blender called "Snap During Transform" that can capture certain points and "magnetize" the mouse cursor to those locations. To enable this tool, you must click on the magnet icon at the 3D Viewport header and choose Vertex from your "Snap To" options (Figure 3.17).

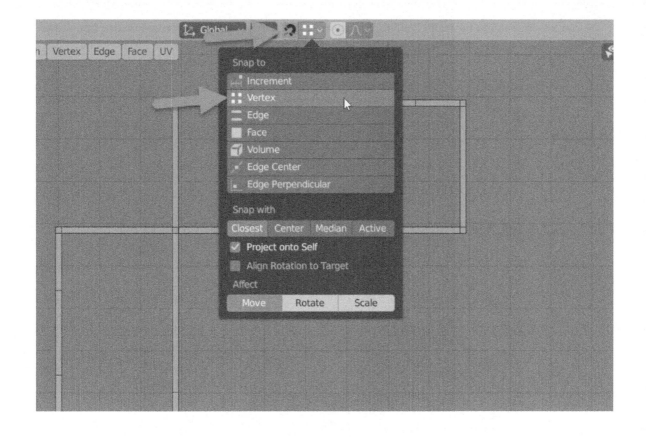

Figure 3.17 - Snap during transform

After enabling the magnet icon, you will notice a small circle will appear whenever you try to apply a transformation to an object (Figure 3.18).

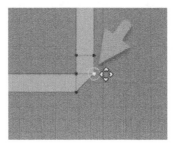

Figure 3.18 - Snap circle

That is a visual indicator of the snap magnetizing all transformations. It will capture vertices close to the mouse cursor and make any transformation to align with those points.

We can use the snap to create all walls from the room on the right quickly. First, select the edge shown in Figure 3.19.

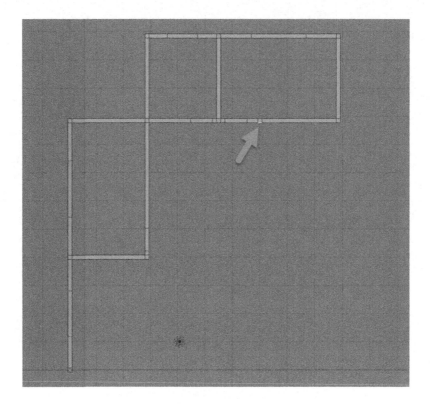

Figure 3.19 - *Selected edge*

Press the E key to extrude, and after that, the Y key. It will constraint the extrude to the Y-axis. Move your mouse cursor near the point shown in Figure 3.20. Once you see the circle at that location, click with the left mouse button to confirm.

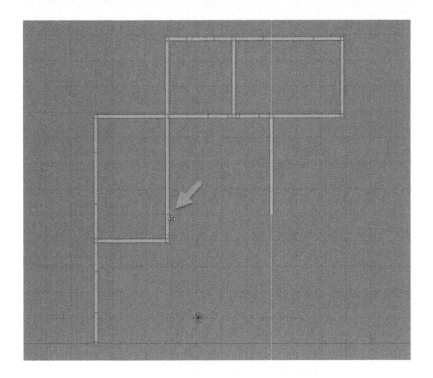

Figure 3.20 - *Captured point*

You will have a wall with the same length using only your mouse as a reference for modeling. That is an incredibly fast way to create 3D models in Blende if you have existing geometry to use as a reference. Using the remaining points in the wall, you can create the next three extrudes (Figure 3.21).

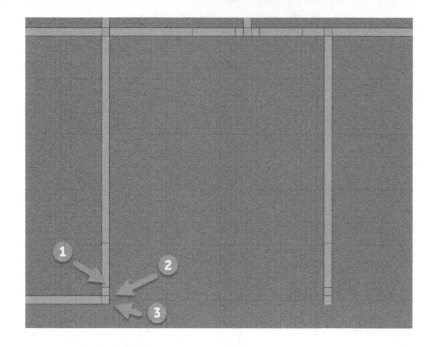

Figure 3.21 - *Next three points to extrude*

With the Snap During transform enabled, select the edge shown in Figure 3.22 to start a new sequence of extrudes.

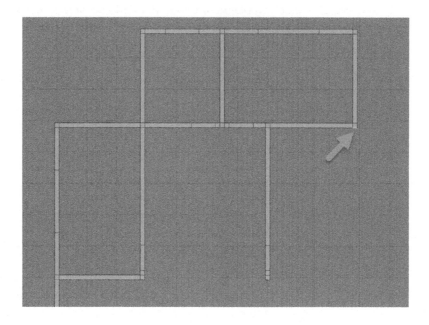

Figure 3.22 - *Selected edge on the right*

Press the E key and the Y key to start an extrude on the Y-axis. Use points from opposite sides of your project to build all parts on the right side of your room (Figure 3.23).

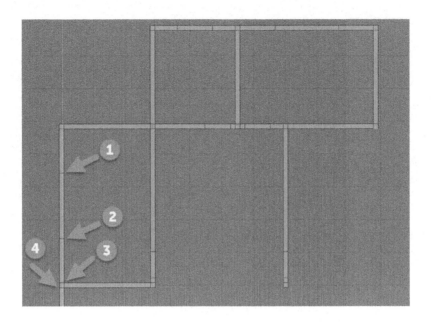

Figure 3.23 - Points to use in the Snap during transform

To finish this modeling process, you can get the two parallel edges at the bottom of this room and press the F key to connect them both. That was a quick and easy way to create a room, which you can use when existing geometry shares the same lengths.

Don't forget to disable the Snap During Transform after using it, or all transformations will start to capture points while you move the mouse.

3.3 Making curved walls

To finish the modeling of our walls, we have to create all the bottom parts of our building, which has a straight wall and also something we still didn't create until now, which is a round shape. To create the wall using an arc, we will have to work with the Spin tool of Blender.

Before starting to use the Spin, we have to create all the remaining walls at the bottom of our floor plan. Select the edge shown in Figure 3.24.

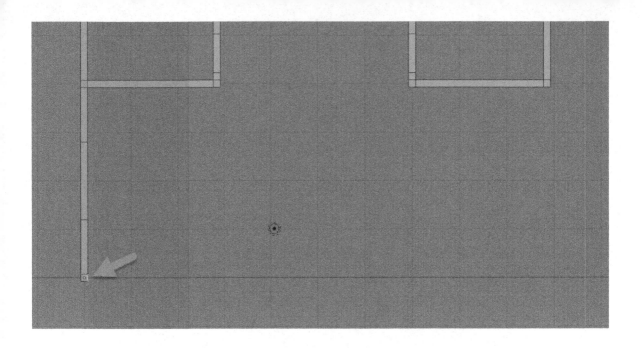

Figure 3.24 - Selected Edge

Start a sequence of extrudes in the X-axis:

1. Press the E key

2. Press the X key

3. Type 1.675

4. Press RETURN to confirm

5. Press the E key

6. Press the X key

7. Type 2.5

8. Press RETURN to confirm

9. Press the E key

10. Press the X key

11. Type 1.675

12. Press RETURN to confirm

From this last extrude, we can start working with the Spin tool, which appears in Edit Mode of Blender at the bottom of your Toolbar (Figure 3.25).

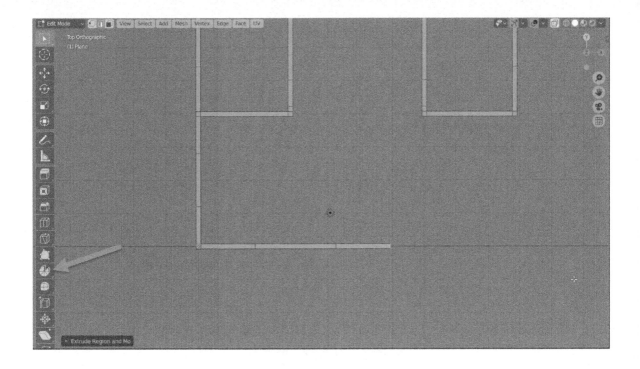

Figure 3.25 - Spin tool

A few important points about the Spin:

– It creates a sequence of copies from a selected vertex or edge and rotate those copies around the 3D Cursor.

– For that reason, you should use the 3D Cursor as the arc center

– The copies created with the Spin will align with your view from the model. Make sure you have an orthographic projection from the top to make a perfect and also orthographic arc or circle.

Based on those points, we must start the drawing of an arc with the 3D Cursor location. How to find the center point for this arc? We can use several methods to measure the length and find the location.

For instance, we can select a vertex from the top right of our wall and using an extrude, and the Snap During Transform create an edge that extends until it reaches the other end of the arc (Figure 3.26).

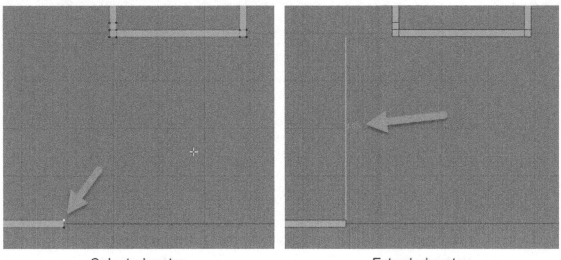

| Selected vertex | Extruded vertex |

Figure 3.26 - *Edge as a reference*

Limit the extrude to the Y-axis and display the length for that edge to find an exact distance. In that case, we got a distance of 3.85 units.

Select the top vertex for the edge created from the extrude. With the vertex still selected, press SHIFT+S and chose "Cursor to Selected" to align your 3D Cursor to the newly created vertex. Once the 3D Cursor is in place, you can delete the reference edge.

With the 3D Cursor at the central location, we are ready to make our Spin. Make sure you are viewing the model from the top and select the edge that will start our arc. Press the Spin tool button, and you will see an arc appearing in the model (Figure 3.27).

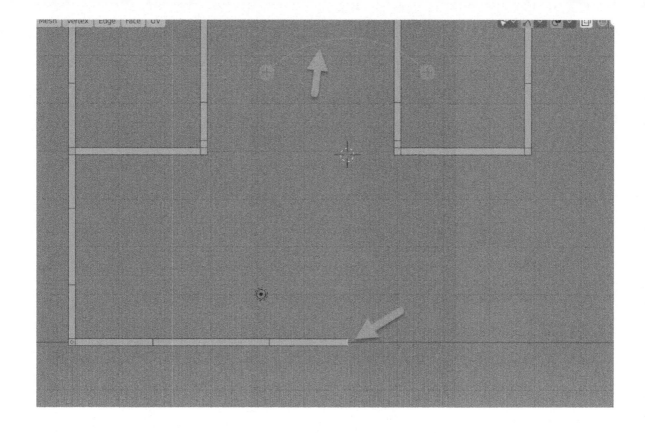

Figure 3.27 - Spin tool arc

Click and drag that arc to start making our round wall. Use the menu that appears on the lower-left corner of the 3D Viewport to adjust the Spin. Use the following settings:

– Angle: -90

– Steps: 32

That will create an arc that has 90 degrees and 32 divisions to make a smooth shaped wall (Figure 3.28).

Figure 3.28 - Curved wall

As the last step for all walls, you can merge all unconnected vertices from the model. Press the A key to select all vertices and press the right mouse button. At the context menu, choose **Merge → By Distance** to remove all unconnected and lose vertices.

3.4 Working with doors and windows

As you probably notice during the drawing process for all walls until this point in the chapter, we also created segments representing doors and windows. You can create those segments at the same time as your walls, but we will have to manage them differently later. Those elements will receive unique settings for line thickness and render in a technical drawing.

Since they are in the correct locations, we have to separate them into new and independent objects. To separate objects in Blender, you can use the P key. In Edit Mode, you should change the selection mode to Faces and select all faces representing a window (Figure 3.29).

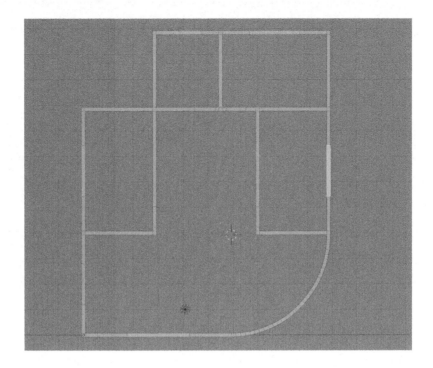

Figure 3.29 - *Windows selected*

After selecting those faces, you can press the P key and choose Selection. That will create a new and unique object for all faces representing windows. Repeat the same process for all doors.

3.5 Drawing the stairs

One of the last missing parts for the floor plan is the small stairs at the entrance of the building, which will allow people to change levels from the entrance hall to the other rooms. The easiest way to draw those stairs is with a sequence of extrudes and the F key to connect both sides of the stairs.

First, select the vertices pointed at Figure 3.30.

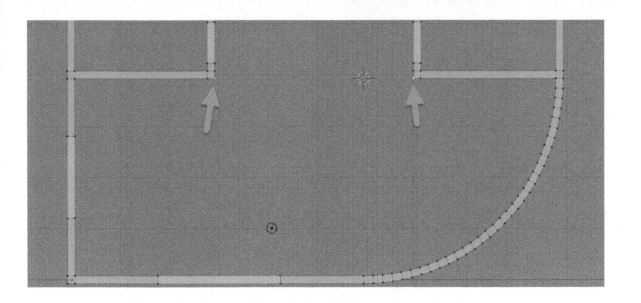

Figure 3.30 - Selected vertices

Create one extrude in the Y-axis:

1. Press the E key

2. Press the Y key

3. Type -0.5

4. Press RETURN to confirm

5. Press the F key

As a result, you will get the first set of steps (Figure 3.31).

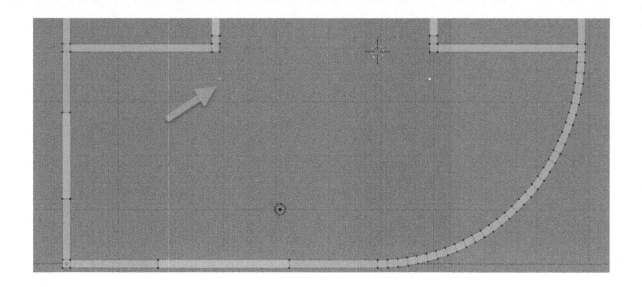

Figure 3.31 - First step

Next, you can use the SHIFT+D key to duplicate each one of the vertical steps 0.25 to each side twice. Also, duplicate the large horizontal edge created with the F key twice (Figure 3.32).

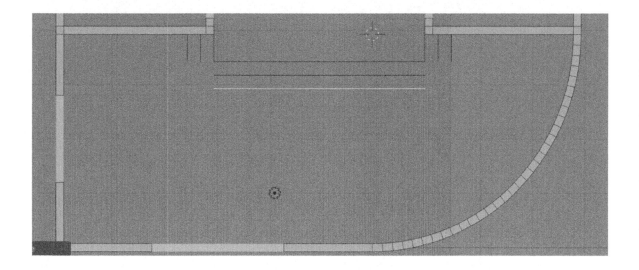

Figure 3.32 - Result after duplicates

Turn on the Snap During Transform, and with the G key, you can move and align each one of the edges to close each shape. For instance, you can select a single vertex and move it on the X-axis. Align with a vertical line and then move the other vertex to close the shape (Figure 3.33).

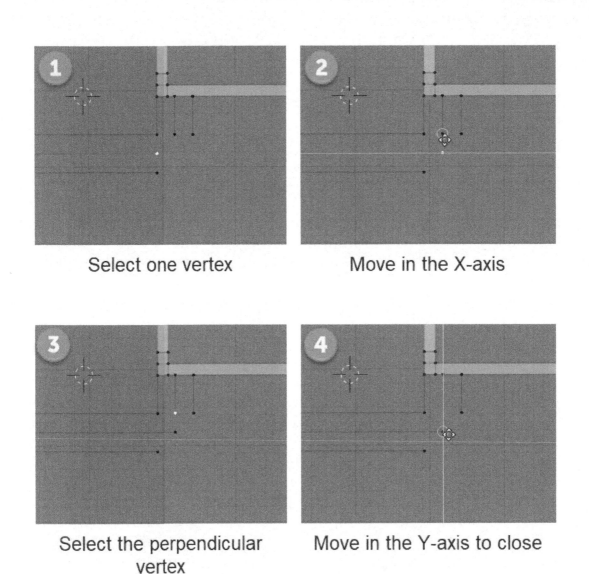

Select one vertex

Move in the X-axis

Select the perpendicular vertex

Move in the Y-axis to close

Figure 3.33 - Closing the shape

Repeat the process with all other parts of the steps until you get the full shape on all stairs.

3.6 Creating the external area

On the top left corner, you will find an area that has a pillar and a space that has a cover not showing up in the floor plan. Later we will have to set up that space with a hidden line. Before that, we must draw both the pillar and area, marking the covered space.

The two objects have a squared shape that makes it easy to draw using a 3D plane. Press the SHIFT+A keys and create a new plane on your scene. Turn on Snap During Transform and move the plane until their bottom right corner captures the vertex shown in Figure 3.34.

Figure 3.34 - *Moving the 3D plane*

Using the snap options, you can resize the 3D plane by selecting each pair of vertices of the object. Select the top two vertices and move them on the Y-axis until it aligns with the wall. Next, move the pair on the left until it also aligned with the wall (Figure 3.35).

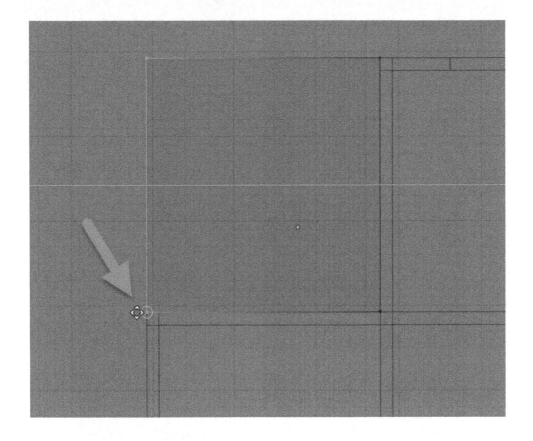

Figure 3.35 - *Moving vertices*

For the pillar, we can either duplicate the 3D plane we created or add a new one using the SHIFT+A keys. The pillar must have 0.4 units on each side. If you decide to create a new plane, you should apply a scale factor of 0.2. Press the S key and type 0.2 (Figure 3.36).

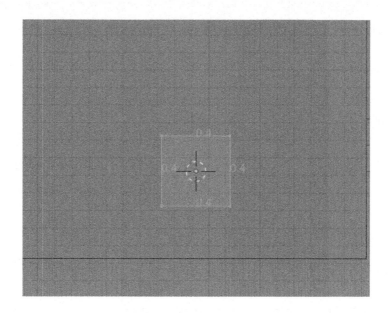

Figure 3.36 - Pillar dimension

Press RETURN to confirm, and in Object Mode, you should also press CTRL+A and choose scale. It will remove the scale factor from the object. The last step with the pillar is to move the object to its final location. Still with the Snap During Transform enabled, you can place the 3D Plane aligned at the top left corner (Figure 3.37).

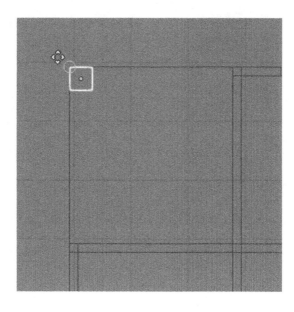

Figure 3.37 - Pillar alignment

Once there, you can move the object 0.2 to the right and 0.2 down:

1. Select the 3D plane

2. Press the G key

3. Press the X key

4. Type 0.2

5. Press RETURN to confirm

6. Press the G key

7. Press the Y key

8. Type -0.2

9. Press RETURN to confirm

And finally, we will have all the elements required to create and set up the floor plan drawing.

3.7 Preparing the floor plan for rendering

Before we start working with the setup process for technical drawings in Blender using the elements created until this point in the chapter, we have to perform one last step if you remember in chapter 2, we explained how to separate drawing elements into Collections.

Those Collections will help us separate and apply unique settings for parts of the drawing. Using the Outliner Editor, you can create the following Collections for the floor plan:

– Walls

– Windows

– Doors

– Viewing

– Hidden

After you create each of the Collections, it is time to organize the model and place each object in their respective Collection. For instance, you can select the objects representing walls and press the M key. From the small menu that will appear, you can choose the Walls Collection (Figure 3.38).

116

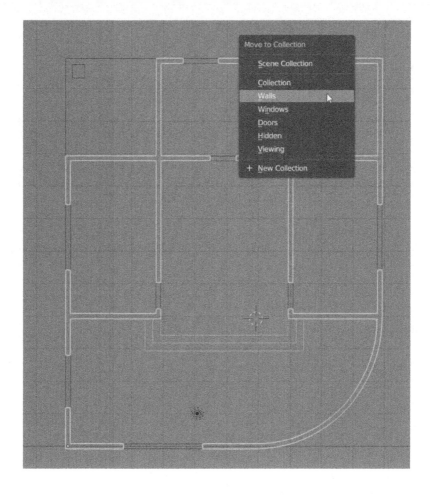

Figure 3.38 - *Walls Collection*

To make your drawing even more organized, you can rename each 3D object in a way that helps you identify them later. For instance, select the Walls object and press F2 in your keyboard. Assign a name like "walls," and you will see it at the Outliner Editor. Repeat the process for all other parts of your floor plan.

What is next?

The drawing process of any 2D shape in Blender has a close relation to 3D modeling because it is a tridimensional object that we are viewing from the top. After creating the walls from our floor plan, you can replicate the same procedure to create all other types of technical drawings using a similar technique.

For instance, after the creation of a floor plan, you might want to start making a section cut for the same building. The procedure required for a section cut works in the same way. You can even use the floor plan design as a reference for later creation.

After the section cut, you can keep producing all the graphical pieces necessary to build an architecture set of technical drawings like an elevation. You now have the basic knowledge to create any 2D shape that will render like a technical drawing.

Chapter 4 - Line Styles and Line Sets

The creation of a technical drawing like a floor plan involves the design of 3D objects that will look like a flat object, and also several settings to make it render like 2D drawing. Now that you have all the base models to start rendering the walls, we can start organizing the project with Line Sets and Styles.

In FreeStyle, you have the Lines Sets that will work like layers from CAD software, which will create "virtual groups" where we can apply unique settings for rendering. You will learn how to create those sets and make them work for a technical drawing.

Connected to each Line Set, you have a style that will determine how the technical drawing will render.

Here is a list of what you will learn:

- Using line settings from FreeStyle

- Working with Line Sets

- Line Styles for technical drawing

- Line Styles for technical drawing

- Line Styles management

- Reusing Line Styles

4.1 Using line settings from FreeStyle

A key component of any technical drawing is the line display that can use several different types and morphologies to represent certain features of a project visually. For instance, you will usually see a thick continuous line for features that you can see in a technical drawing. A dashed thin line will usually represent a hidden feature.

In the previous chapter, we started to create a floor plan that will work as an example of how we can render technical drawings using Blender. Inside the settings for FreeStyle, you will find two groups of options that will help us manage the display of lines:

- Line Set

- Line Style

We already used the Line Set in Chapter 2 in a quick overview of how to start making renderings with FreeStyle for technical drawing. The Line Set will work as a layering system from CAD tools. You will assign a group of objects by Collection to each individual Set and later assign a Line Style.

The purpose of a Line Set is to separate objects by type. You can create a Line Style for each Line Set. With a Line Style, you will effectively control how each line will appear in a render. It will be possible to specify:

- Shape

- Thickness

- Effects

It is possible to share a single Line Style across multiple Line Sets that will represent similar features. In Figure 4.1, you can see a simple way to organize a technical drawing project.

Figure 4.1 - *Line Sets*

From Figure 4.1, you will get a type of object, assign a Line Set to have individual control over their lines, and assign a Line Style to each set. That is the usual workflow needed to organize a technical drawing in Blender.

You will first create the 3D objects and then make a unique Line Set that will group similar features like walls. For that Line Set with walls, you will assign an existing Line Style or create a new one.

4.2 Working with Line Sets

After you have the 3D model ready to receive lines and settings from FreeStyle like the floor plan we created in chapter 3, it is time to add some Line Sets to organize the project. As mentioned before, the main purpose of a Line Set in FreeStyle is to separate all features from a drawing.

The Line Set options are available at the View Layer Properties tab (Figure 4.2).

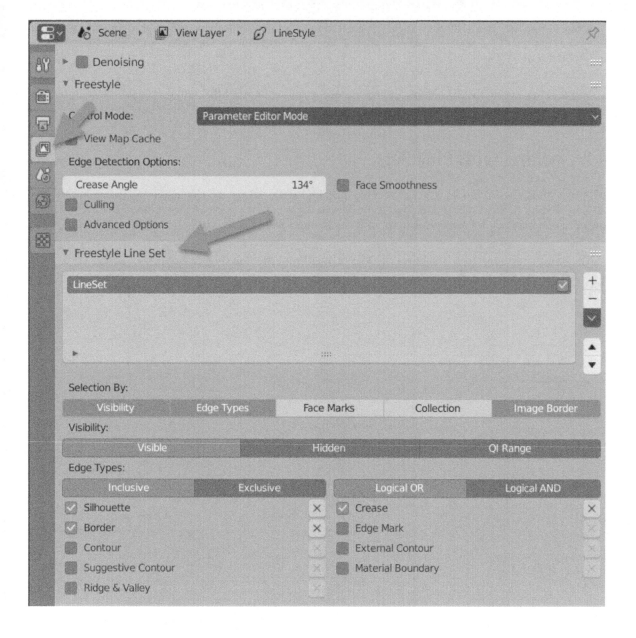

Figure 4.2 - Line Set

A single project in Blender can use multiple Line Sets for a drawing, which will depend on the number of features you have to separate from each other. In the floor plan we can usually create a small list of features:

– Walls

– Windows

- Doors

- Viewing

- Hidden

Later we can add more Line Sets for annotation, symbols, and dimension lines. By now, we can start using those features to create Line Sets. To make your life easier and quickly adjust all objects, it is a good practice to start by making a Collection for each one of the features.

With a Collection, you can assign a Line Set to control those objects and later include new elements by simply making them a part of each Collection.

You can start making the Collections in the Outliner Editor with a right-click and choosing "New" (Figure 4.3).

Figure 4.3 - Creating a new Collection

Once you create the Collection, it is imperative to assign a name that will help you identify the group. For instance, use the same name for each feature. In the Collection for Walls, use the "Walls" as the name (Figure 4.4).

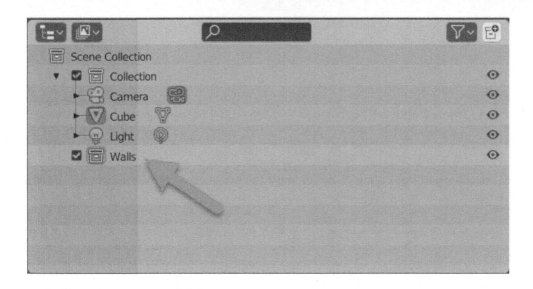

Figure 4.4 - Collection name

To rename a Collection, you can double-click on any existing name.

After you create the Collections, it is time to move each object to the proper Collection. You can move them in two ways:

– Select the object and press the M key. From the list, you will choose the Collection you wish to use by their name.

– At the Outliner Editor, you can click and drag the object by name to the Collection.

Regardless of the method you choose, it is essential to get each object in a unique Collection.

After moving each object for the floor plan, we will have the following organization of Collections and objects in the Outliner Editor (Figure 4.5).

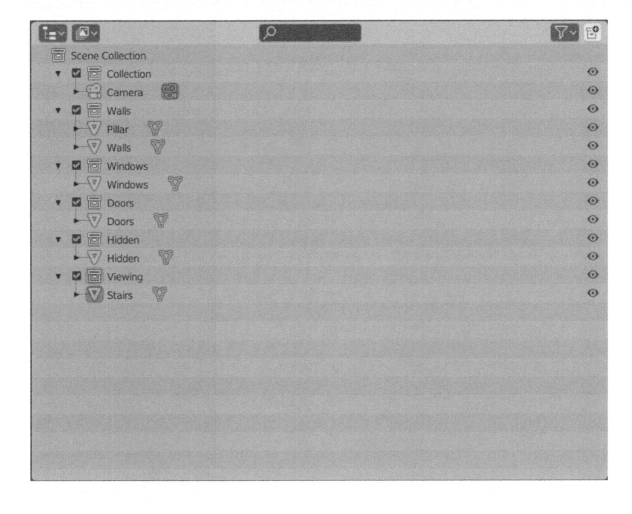

Figure 4.5 - *Collections in Outliner*

That will work for the floor plan model, which you will have to adapt for each type of technical drawing you plan to create in Blender.

Tip: *As a way to further organize the scene with Collections, you can also make nested Collections. For instance, you can create a collection for different types of annotation and make another that will hold all those subtypes. To nest a Collection, you can click and drag an existing collection and release it over an existing Collection.*

4.2.1 Creating Line Sets for technical drawing

After the creation of Collections for each one of the features in the project, it is time to start making Line Sets. You can follow the same names and features for each Line Set.

You can add and remove Line Sets using the "+" and "-"buttons on the right side of your "FreeStyle Line Set" options. There you will also find an option do copy and paste existing Line Sets. Using the small button bellow "-"you will show options to copy and paste a Line Set (Figure 4.6).

Figure 4.6 - *Copy and paste a Line Set*

It is also possible to disable a Line Set to remove them from a render by disabling the checkbox next to the Line Set name. Once you disable the Line Set, all objects using that set will stop appearing in your render.

For each Collection, you should create a Line Set (Figure 4.7).

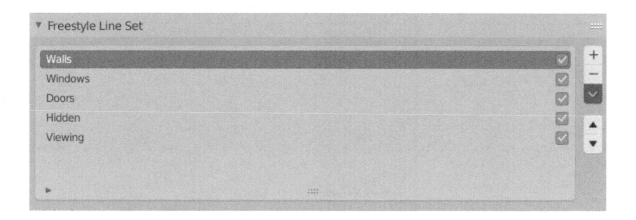

Figure 4.7 - *Line Sets*

Once you have all the Line Sets for the drawing, we can start using them to assign the object groups.

4.2.2 Filtering objects by type and Collection

For each one of the Line Sets, we will have to connect them with the Collection that has the same features needed for rendering. For instance, we can take the Line Set with the name of Walls. Select that line Set from the list and enable the Collection option at the "Selection By" field.

You will see a selector for the Collection appearing at the bottom of your Line Set field. There you will click and choose the Collection that has your walls model (Figure 4.8).

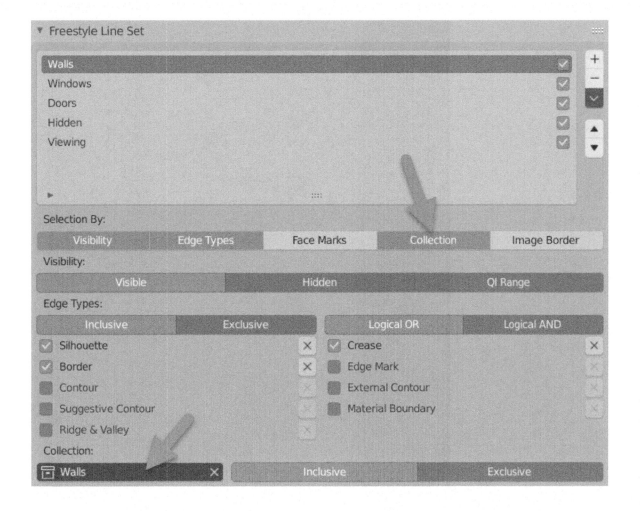

Figure 4.8 - *Collection for walls*

As the last step to ensure we have only the edges necessary for the technical drawing, we can select the wall model and add some FreeStyle Edge Marks. In Edit Mode, select all the edges you wish to use for rendering. If you are in Edge selection mode, use a right-click to open the context menu and choose "Mark FreeStyle Edge" (Figure 4.9).

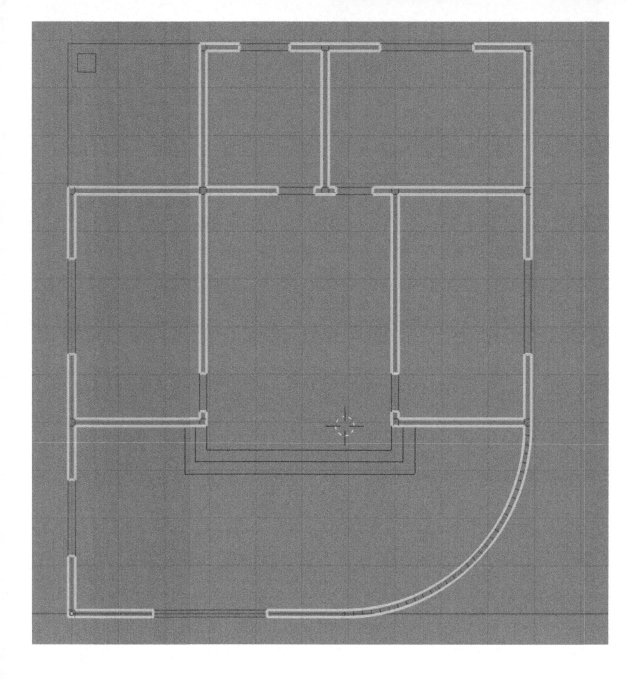

Figure 4.9 - *Walls with marks*

Once you have the edges with a FreeStyle Mark, you can go to the Line Set options for the Walls, and from your "Edge Types" options, disable all features but the Edge Mark (Figure 4.10).

Figure 4.10 - *Edge Types options*

It will ensure we only have the edges from the walls that we need will appear in the final render.

With the Line Set for walls ready, we can make a quick render to ensure everything is working properly. Assuming you have the same settings described in chapter 2 with a camera pointing from the top and in orthographic mode, you will see the floor plan walls rendered as Figure 4.11.

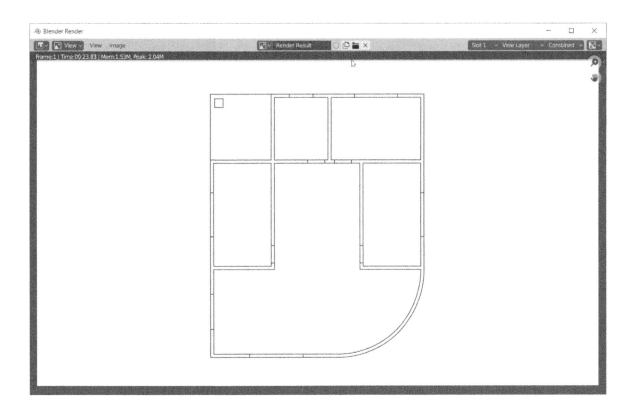

Figure 4.11 - *Floor plan rendering preview*

We still have to make lots of small adjustments to the lines and other features from the floor plan. The next step is to assign all other Collections to the respective Line Sets. For each object, you will also add "Mark FreeStyle Edge" in all edges you want to appear at the final render.

In summary, you can perform the Line Set preparations in the following order:

1. Create Collections for each feature of your technical drawing

2. Add the objects to the respective Collection

3. Create the Line Sets for each feature

4. Assign a Collection to each Line Set

5. Add the "Mark FreeStyle Edge" to all edges you want to appear at the final render

6. Change settings from line Sets to use only your Edge Marks to display strokes

You can anticipate step five from the list during the modeling stage and start your Line Set configuration with all the marls already in place. Regardless of the order, you choose to follow; it will result in a model ready to receive Line Styles for all parts of your technical drawing.

Tip: You can create as many Line Sets you need to help you create a technical drawing. For instance, a project could have multiple types of walls that will require unique settings for lines. In that case, you can create a Line Set to each kind.

4.3 Line Styles for technical drawing

Unlike the Line Sets that will work as an organizational option for FreeStyle, you will set up the looks of every line in a render using Line Styles. A style can control lots of aspects related to your drawing, including:

– Shape

– Thickness

– Color

– Transparency

The Line Styles works like a material that you can apply to a 3D Model but for lines in FreeStyle. You can create and manage Line Styles using the selector at the top of your "FreeStyle Line Style" menu (Figure 4.12).

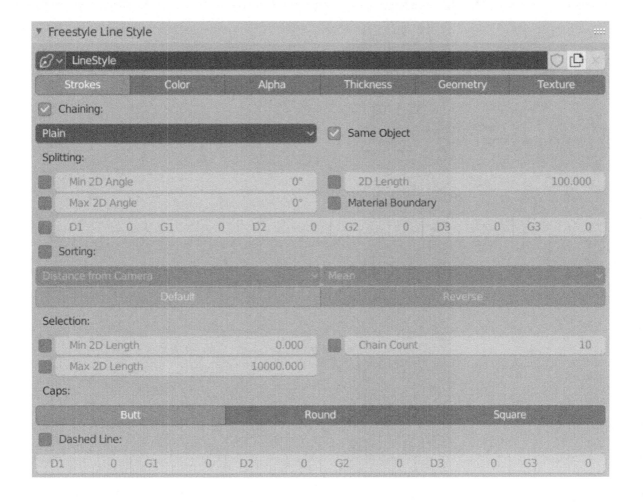

Figure 4.12 - *Line Style options*

Each Line Style can receive a unique name, which you can change by clicking at the "LineStyle" to re-name. You can also choose an existing Line Style in the same file you are working by clicking in the small pen icon (Figure 4.13).

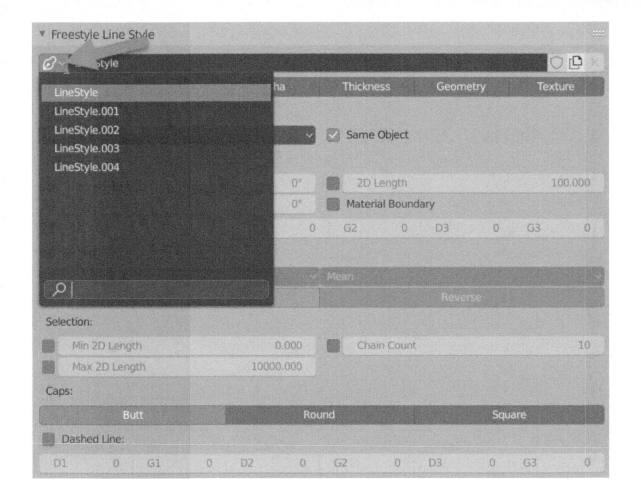

Figure 4.13 - Pen icon

It will list all available Line Styles in your file. Regarding Line Style names, it is a good practice to assign a name that helps you identify the type of line it will generate. For instance, you can use a name like "SolidContinuous0.5" that will give you shape, type, and thickness.

At the top of your Line Style options you will see sections where you can make adjustments for six main aspects of your Line Style:

– Strokes

– Color

– Alpha

– Thickness

– Geometry

– Texture

For technical drawings, you will usually work with only the first four options to set up the visuals for each feature.

4.3.1 Line Style strokes

The first thing that we can adjust in a Line Style is the Stroke tab, which will let you control each line in your technical drawing. If you need a continuous straight line, you don't have to make significant changes from the default options (Figure 4.14).

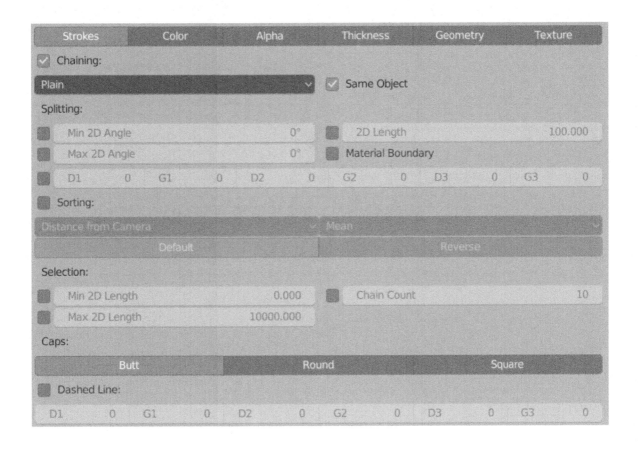

Figure 4.14 - *Stroke options*

One aspect of the drawing that you will control in the Strokes is the creation of dashed lines. If you need that type of line it will be necessary to enable "Dashed Line" at the bottom of your options (Figure 4.15).

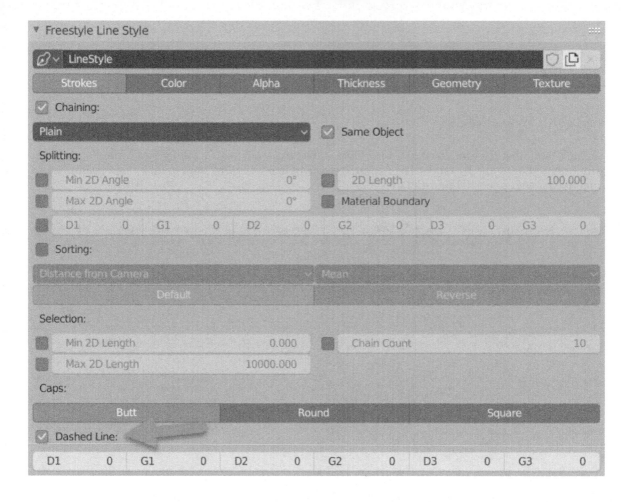

Figure 4.15 - Dashed line options

There you will have to use the values to control how you want the dashes. For instance, you will see a sequential set of values:

- **D1**: Dash length 1

- **G1**: Gap length 1

- **D2**: Dash length 2

- **G2**: Gap length 2

- **D3**: Dash length 3

- **G3**: Gap length 3

For instance, if you use a value of 10 for dash and 6 for the gap in all fields, you will get a dashed line, as shown in Figure 4.16.

Figure 4.16 - Dashed line results

Those values will have to change based on the scale and camera distance to the object.

4.3.2 Line Style Color, Alpha, and thickness

With the next two sections, you will get controls to change some basic aspects of the strokes like color and thickness. The options here are simple to use and understand, where you get a clot picker for the color panel (Figure 4.17).

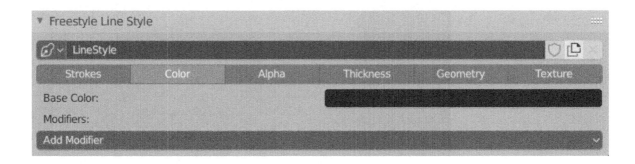

Figure 4.17 - *Color options*

At the color options, you will be able to select a unique color or gradient for the entire Line Style. For technical drawings that will use a white background with black lines, you don't have to change anything from the default settings. However, you can also create an inverted image by using a black background with white lines or any other color you prefer.

For the Alpha settings, you can use transparency for each one of the lines using a simple slider. When the value is at one, you will have an opaque line, and a value of zero will give a fully transparent line.

The same simple slider applies to thickness, which is a setting for Line Styles that we will use a lot in technical drawing. Since those drawings will require you to create multiple lines with the specific thickness you will have to create a Line Style for each line requiring a unique thickness (Figure 4.18).

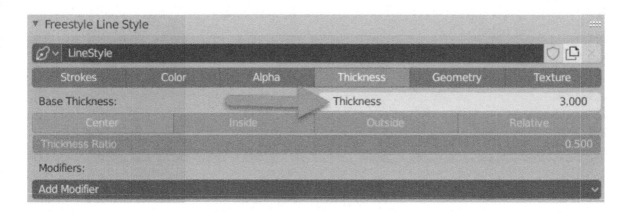

Figure 4.18 - *Line Thickness*

At the Thickness options, you will also find options to choose where you want to start counting the thickness:

– Center

– Inside

– Outside

– Relative

The default option is to use your line center as the base to add thickness to the objects.

4.3.3 Line Style Geometry and Textures

With the last two options in Line Styles, you will get settings to change the geometry of your lines and also apply a texture to them. Unless you want to make a stylized version of a technical drawing, it is unlikely that those options will apply to such projects.

For instance, we can use the Geometry section to apply a modifier called Backbone Stretcher (Figure 4.19).

Figure 4.19 - *Backbone Stretcher*

It will create tips at the end of each of your lines. The modifier list in the Geometry section will offer other unique visual effects for lines. For a more traditional technical drawing, you will probably avoid such type of modification.

4.4 Line Styles for technical drawing

After the overview of each Line Style setting for technical drawings, it is time to create some Line Styles for the floor plan. To keep the drawing organized, we will create the styles using names that will help us identify each property later.

From the list of features in the floor plan, we will need styles for the following objects with the respective name for each LineStyle:

- **Walls**: ContinousLine-3.0

- **Windows**: ContinousLine-2.0

- **Doors**: ContinousLine-2.0

- **Viewing**: ContinousLine-1.0

- **Hidden**: DashedLine-0.75

To create the first Line Style, we can use the Walls Line Set. Select that Line Set, and we can create a new Line Style by clicking at the icon on the right of each Line Style name (Figure 4.20).

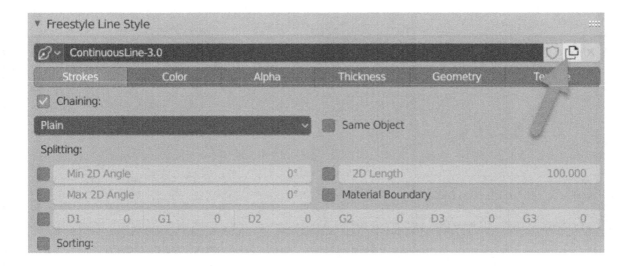

Figure 4.20 - Creating a new Line Style

Rename that Line Style as "ContinousLine-3.0," and since we are using a continuous straight line, you can keep the Stroke tab with the default settings. Both Color and Alpha can also use the default options. At the thickness, you will change the base value to 3.0 (Figure 4.21).

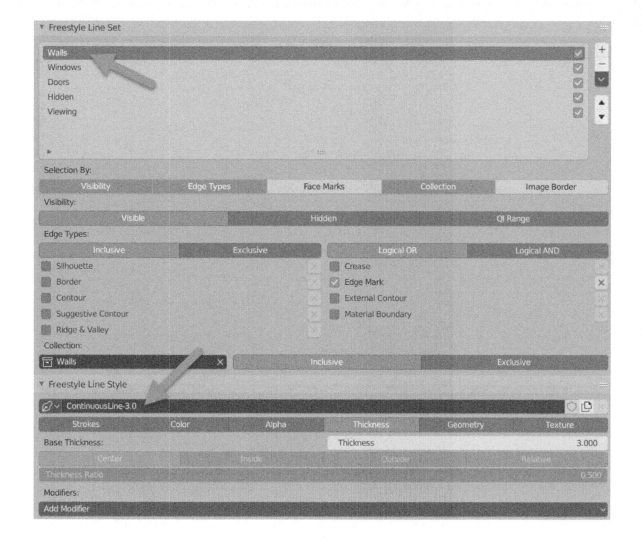

Figure 4.21 - *Thickness value*

If you render the scene now, you will see the walls with a continuous straight line using 3.0 as thickness (Figure 4.22).

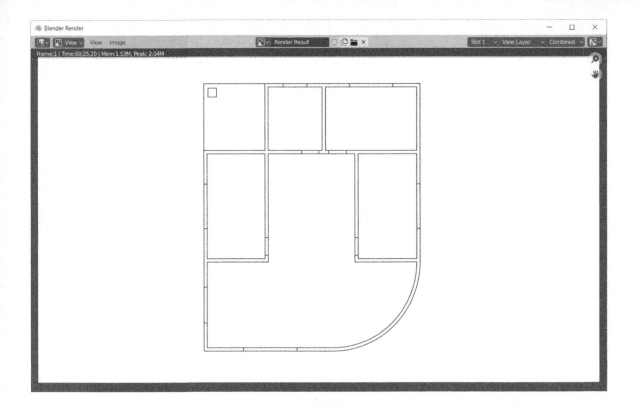

Figure 4.22 - *Walls rendering*

You can repeat the same steps to create unique Line Styles for all remaining Line Sets. The settings for Windows, Doors, and Viewing will use the same options with the only difference in thickness.

The Hidden Line Style will use a dashed line, which you will enable in the Stroke section and use a value of two and one for the dash and gap, respectively (Figure 4.23).

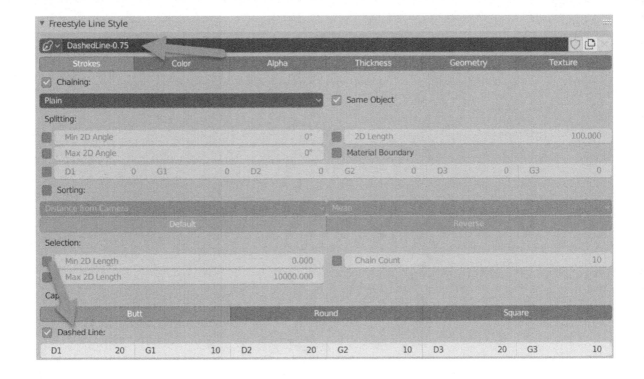

Figure 4.23 - *Dashed line settings*

You can use the same settings for Color, Alpha, and Thickness, as the Line Style name describes. If you press F12 to render the floor plan now, you will see something that is starting to look like a technical drawing (Figure 4.24).

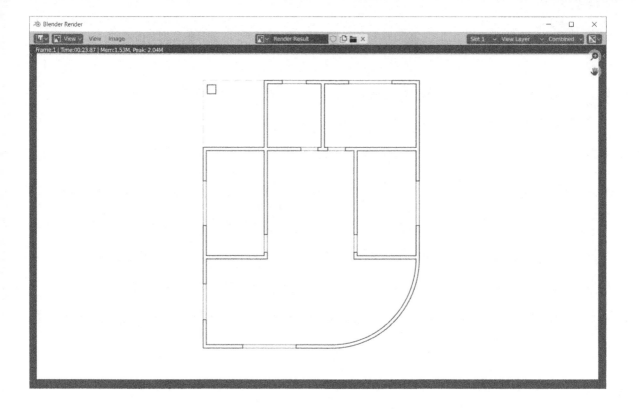

Figure 4.24 - *Floor plan with Line Styles*

After you add Line Styles to the drawing, you will see different thicknesses for each feature in the technical drawing, which will make it look a lot more like something you can use to describe a project.

4.5 Line Styles management

A typical project in Blender will use several Line Styles to create a better technical drawing using Free-Style. With so many Line Styles in a project, it is critical to find ways to manage and organize them in a way you can easily select and eventually remove unused styles.

On the right side of the Line Style name, you will find controls that will help us manage the styles (Figure 4.25).

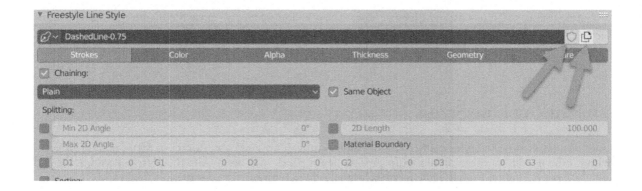

Figure 4.25 - *Line Styles controls*

The middle icon will duplicate an existing Line Style to create a new one based on the current style. You will notice that the last icon with the "x" is not available. Since you can't have a Line Set that doesn't feature a Line Style, you can't erase a style.

To erase a style, you must create a new one and make sure no other Line Set from the file is using that particular style. When a style doesn't have any Line Set using it, you will see a zero next to their name in the Line Style selector (Figure 4.26).

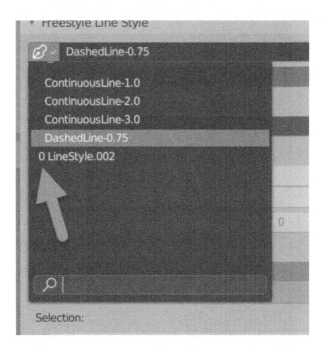

Figure 4.26 - *Line Style Selector*

A style that is not in use by any Line Set is set for exclusion when you close the Blender file. If you want to keep that style in the project even with no Line Sets using it, you will have to enable a Fake User. The icon with a small shield will enable the Fake User, which prevents the style from disappearing if you close Blender.

4.6 Reusing Line Styles

Once you have the Line Styles ready to render any technical drawing, you can reuse them in other projects without the need to perform all the setup process again. Since they are a Data Block from Blender, we can use the Append option from the File menu to transfer them between Blender files.

After making all Line Styles for a particular project, you should save the Blender file in your hard drive. Create a new Blender project using the **File → New** menu to start a new project and then open the **File → Append** menu. It will open the Blender file picker where you should locate the file that has all Line Styles saved. Select that file and hit "Open."

It will display a list of Folders for that file with a list of Data Blocks you can bring to the current Blender file. One of the folders has the name of "Line Styles" (Figure 4.27).

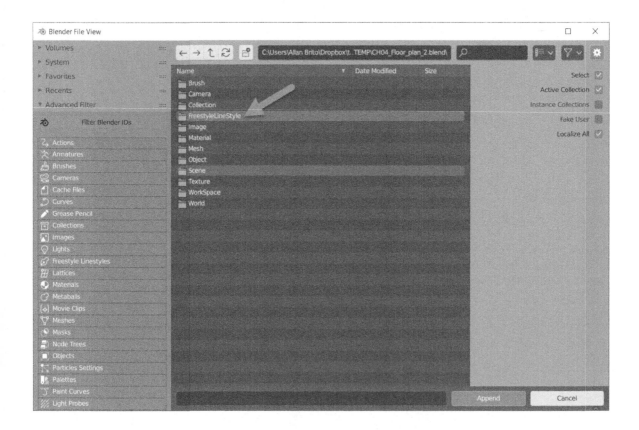

Figure 4.27 - Line Styles folder

Select the Line Styles you want to transfer from the list and press the "Append" button. It will bring your Line Styles with all settings ready to use in a new technical drawing. If you are using the advice on naming each Line Style, you have a quick way to identify how each style will interact with a Line Set.

What is next?

The FreeStyle settings from Blender will allow creating all kinds of projects and stylized renders by adding strokes to objects in your scene. If you design the objects as we did in chapter 2, the results will be a technical drawing. Since a technical drawing had strict rules about line thickness and display, you should always try to maintain a pattern for your Line Sets.

As a next step to develop even further your skills, you should try to make updates to the thickness and styles of each line for different scales. Select the orthographic camera from your project and make changes to the Orthographic Scale. Set values for the thickness and dashed lines, and start rendering.

Make a closer render to a room and adjust the Line Styles. Also, you can start saving the Line Style from your project to reuse.

Chapter 5 - Doors, Windows, and CAD Blocks

The drawing we created in the last chapter has a lot of elements that still make it look like a technical drawing. You already have lines rendering with different thickness settings and also a precise control on what objects we have to render.

However, a few objects are still needing work like doors and windows. For windows, we will have to add the frame representation, which is simple to create and replicate. The object that will give us some extra work is the doors. Usually, a door in a floor plan has the object representing the door itself and also an arc.

That arc will point the way our door will open in the project. We will have to create a process to render only the arc object for each door.

Here is a list of what you will learn in the chapter:

- How to fix the stairs objects that are not rendering

- Adding a frame to each window

- Creating doors and arcs

- Adjusting the arc and door origin points

- Duplicating and mirroring the doors

- Using FreeStyle settings to render only the arc

- Creating a double-sided door

- Importing CAD blocks

- Converting CAD blocks to use in Blender

- Cleaning up CAD blocks for FreeStyle

5.1 Fixing the stairs

If you take a close look at the render from our floor plan until this point in the book, you will notice that despite having geometry to represent the stairs connecting the reception area and hall, we still don't see any strokes. To add those strokes, we have to make sure all objects have a polygon face and not only an edge.

That is a simple rule you must follow for all elements in Blender if you have plans to create 2D Drawings. To use FreeStyle and render strokes in any object, you must have that object with a 3D Face. Unlike all other objects in our project, we have the stairs with only edges and no faces.

To fix those stairs, we have to add some 3D faces to all steps. Since the geometry already exists, the process is easy and involves selecting four vertices of the model in Edit Mode (Figure 5.1).

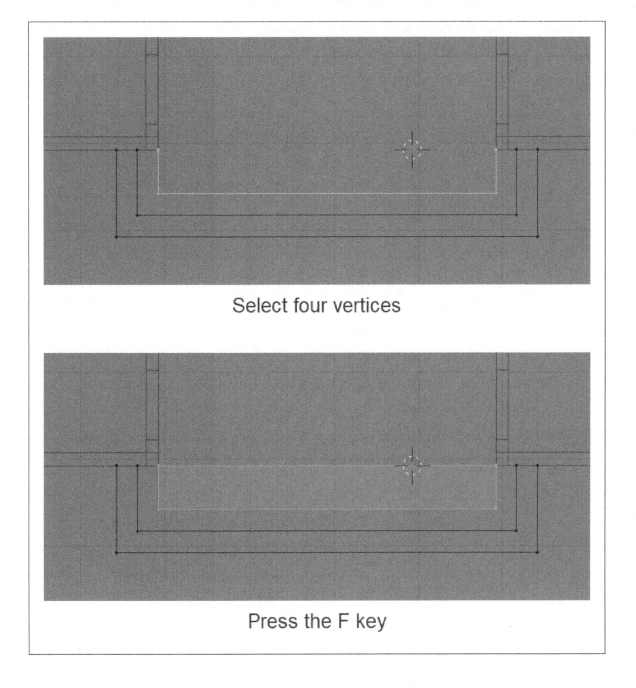

Figure 5.1 - *Selecting vertices to create a face*

Still in Edit Mode, you can press the F key once you select all four vertices. It will connect all of the vertices with a plane. You can repeat the process for all other steps. You must have three large rectangles representing the stairs. If you try to render them now, you won't see any stairs yet.

We still have to add the FreeStyle Edge Mark to the locations where we need to see strokes. In Edit Mode, make sure you are in edge select mode, and with the left mouse button, you can select the edges shown in Figure 5.2.

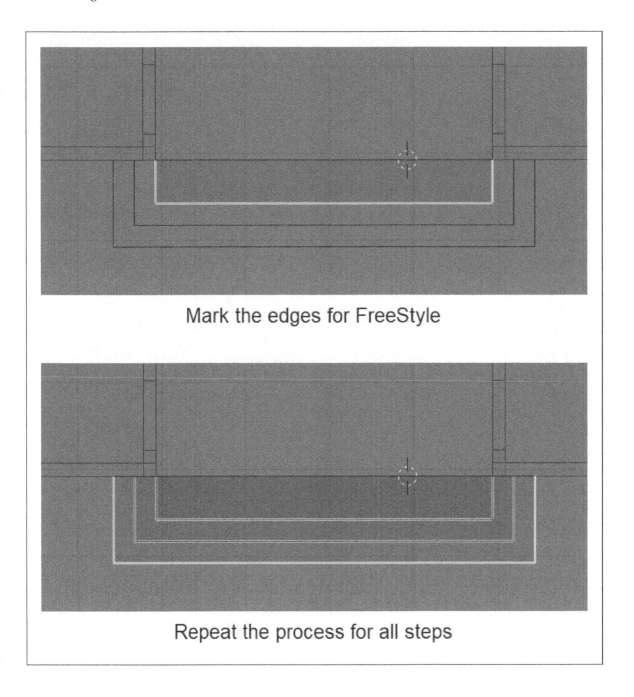

Mark the edges for FreeStyle

Repeat the process for all steps

Figure 5.2 - Selected edges

Using the right mouse button, you can choose the "Mark FreeStyle Edge" from the context menu. In Figure 5.2, you will also see the final result after marking all necessary edges to represent each step.

If you make a render of the project now, you will see the steps appearing (Figure 5.3).

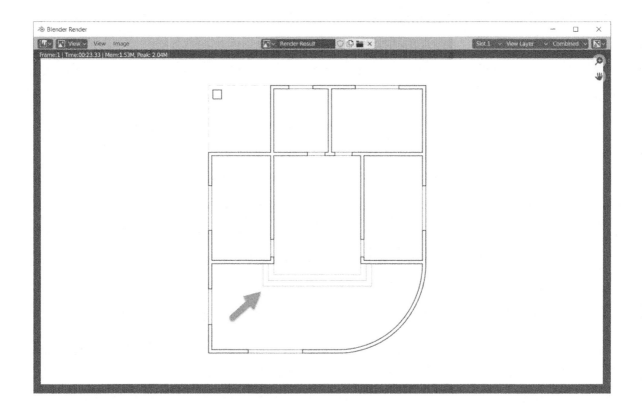

Figure 5.3 - Render with all steps

Since the steps are already in a Collection that has a Line Set and Line Style, you don't need any changes to the objects regarding those settings. It is only a matter of adding the 3D faces to make them appear in the render.

Tip: If you still don't see any strokes from your stairs, it may indicate that come vertices of your object still don't form a closed shape. In that case, you can select all vertices from a step and press the right mouse button. There you will use the Merge → By Distance option to remove any duplicates and unconnected vertices. The option appears in Edit Mode when you are selecting vertices.

5.2 Adding a frame to windows

Another aspect of the floor plan that also needs some work is the drawing of all windows. In the technical drawing, it is common to represent the frames of windows using two parallel lines in the middle of a window. The drawing we have at the moment doesn't have those lines, and we can easily add them to the project.

You can choose any window object to start adding the lines. The process of adding the lines is the same for all windows, and once you learn how to create one, it will be easy to replicate the technique to all other windows.

The technique uses a combination of:

- Snap tool (SHIFT+S)

- 3D Cursor

- Scale transformation (S key)

- Pivot point control

You can start by selecting the window object, which has all the windows from the floor plan and enters Edit Mode. There you will select all vertices from a single window. You can use:

- **B Key**: Draw a window around the vertices you want to select

- **CTRL+L keys**: Select one vertex and press those keys to select all connected vertices

- **ALT+A**: Remove all objects from the selection in case you have to start over

Once you select all the vertices of a window, you must align the 3D Cursor to the selection. Press the SHIFT+S keys and choose "Cursor to Selected" (Figure 5.4).

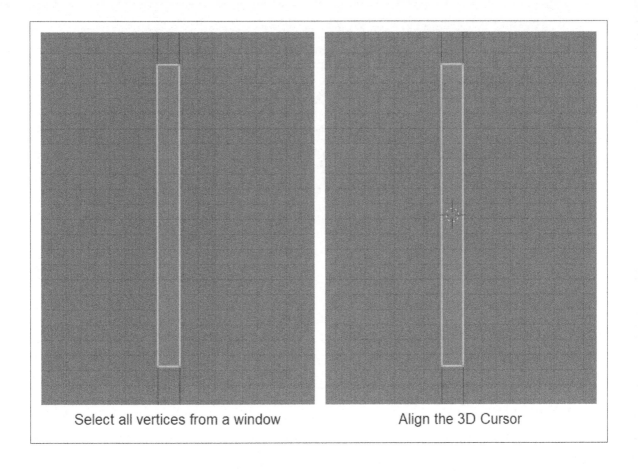

| Select all vertices from a window | Align the 3D Cursor |

Figure 5.4 - *Selecting and aligning the 3D Cursor*

That will make your 3D Cursor to align with the selected vertices. With the cursor at the center of your selection, we can use it as a pivot point for transformations like a scale. Change the pivot point mode at the 3D Viewport header to use the 3D Cursor (Figure 5.5).

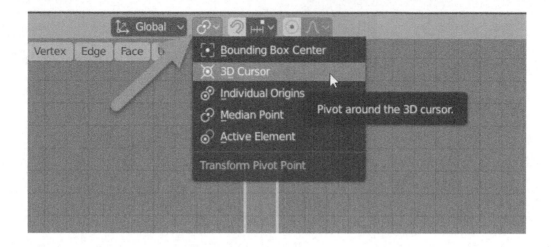

Figure 5.5 - Pivot point mode

The technique now involves the creation of a duplicate from our existing window object:

1. Press the SHIFT+D keys

2. Press ESC to cancel any transformations to the copied object

3. Press the S key

4. Press the X key

5. Type 0.25

6. Press RETURN to confirm

You should see a smaller rectangular shape in the middle of your selected window (Figure 5.6).

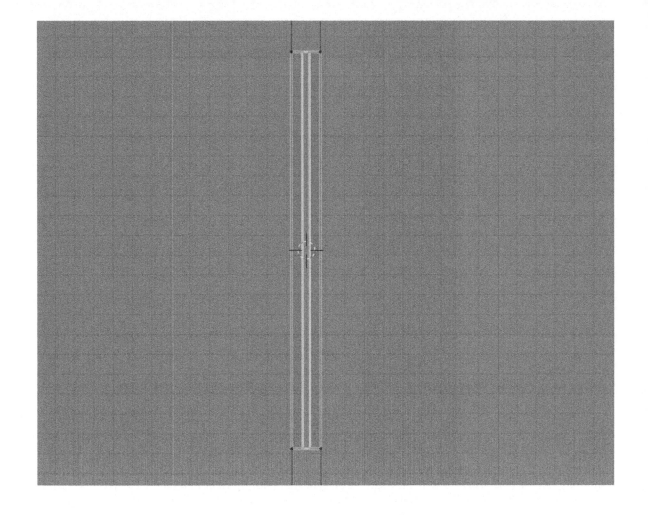

Figure 5.6 - *Window with frame*

The copied object should appear in your scene with the necessary FreeStyle Edge mark, but if it doesn't appear in your render, you can always select the object and with a right-click, add the marks. Now, you can repeat the same process to all other windows in the scene, and you will get them ready for render (Figure 5.7).

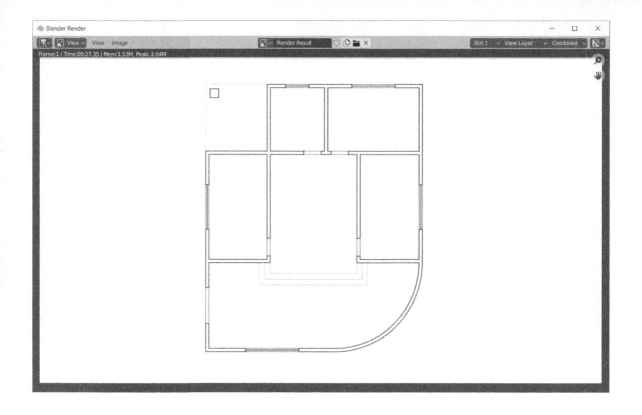

Figure 5.7 - *Windows with frames*

Notice that you will have to make a small adjustment to the process, depending on the window orientation. The example described is a vertical window, and for that reason, we applied the scale in the X-axis. If you have a horizontal window, you will have to apply the scale on the Y-axis.

5.3 Creating doors and arcs

A technical drawing will usually require a unique type of representation for windows and also doors. At the moment, all doors from our floor plan have a rectangular shape that doesn't look like the code you find in technical drawings. Usually, you get a rectangular shape and either an arc or straight line showing the direction in which the door opens.

The next step in our floor plan drawing is to add the correct representation to all doors. It will use a similar approach from the windows, where we will apply a scale to the object and use the 3D Cursor to manage pivot points.

You can begin the process by selecting the doors object and going to Edit Mode. There you must set the selection mode to vertex and select all vertices from a single door object. After selecting the vertices:

1. Press the SHIFT+S key

2. Choose "Cursor to Selected"

3. Press the S key

4. Press the X key

5. Type 0.25

6. Press RETURN to confirm

The sequence will work if you have the pivot point settings using the 3D Cursor (Figure 5.8).

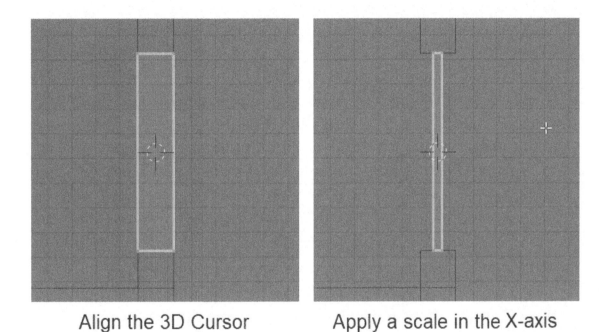

Align the 3D Cursor   Apply a scale in the X-axis

Figure 5.8 - *Door object*

We now have the door model created, and it is time to apply a rotation to "open" the door. Before we do that out is necessary to move our 3D Cursor once again. Select the vertices shown in Figure 5.9, which is the bottom left vertex of your door. Once you select the vertex, press the SHIFT+S keys, and choose "Cursor to Selected."

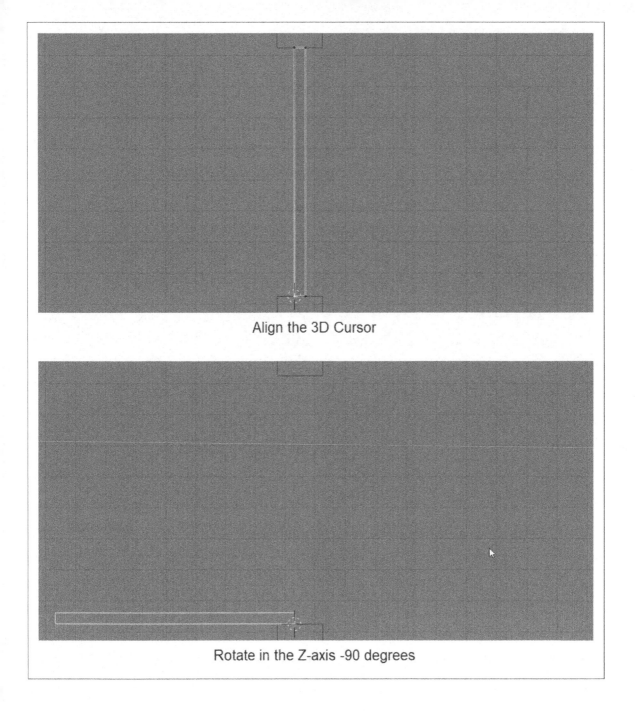

Figure 5.9 - *Rotating the door*

Press the CTRL+L keys to select all connected vertices of your door and apply a rotation:

1. Press the R key

2. Press the Z key

3. Type -90

4. Press RETURN to confirm

That sequence will rotate your door object minus 90 degrees in the Z-axis and place it in an "open state." Depending on the door you select from the floor plan, you may have to change the rotation angle and also the location for your 3D Cursor.

The example used in this section takes a vertical door that opens to the left.

5.3.1 Drawing the arc for doors

One of the challenges related to drawing a door in Blender is that you must represent an arc showing the opening path for each door. That a common visual representation for any technical drawing. To create the arc, we have to keep in mind the same ruled for all objects that must show a stroke in Blender. The object must have 3D faces and not only edges.

As a strategy to create those arcs, we will use the Spin tool again, which we already used back in chapter 3. As a starting point, you can keep the 3D Cursor aligned with the same vertex used to rotate the door. Also, select the top-left vertex from the door object (Figure 5.10).

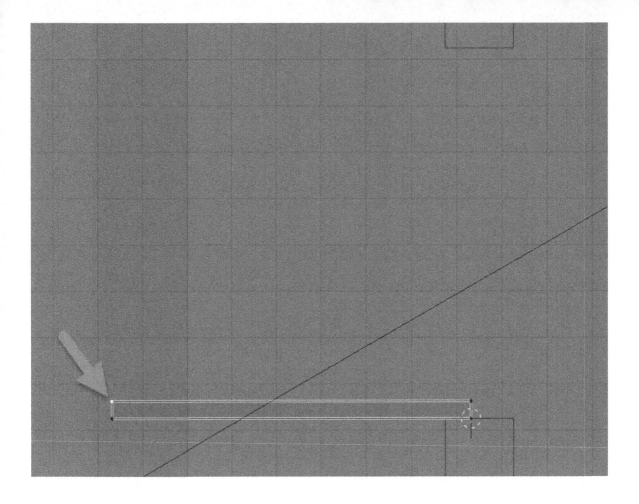

Figure 5.10 - *Selecting a door vertex*

If you don't remember how to the Spin tool works:

– It takes any selected object and makes multiple copies by rotating them around the 3D Cursor

– The Spin creates a shape by connecting each copy

– You can edit details about the Spin in the small menu that appears at the lower-left corner of your 3D Viewport

Once you have the vertex selected, you can press the Spin tool button at the Toolbar. A blue arc will appear on top of your object. Click and drag your mouse cursor above the arc, and you will start to see the arc appearing (Figure 5.11).

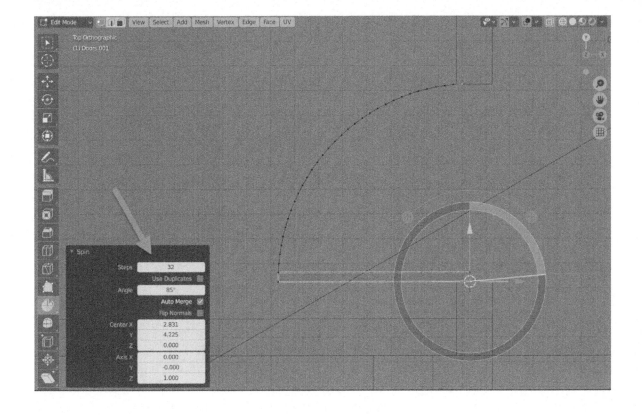

Figure 5.11 - *Spin tool arc*

Change the settings for your Spin tool to use 32 Steps and 85 degrees as the Angle. You should have an arc that shows the opening direction for your door. However, if you start a render now, your arc will not appear with any strokes because it is only a sequence of edges. We have to add 3D faces to make it appear in a render.

Align the 3D Cursor with the top-right vertex of your door (Figure 5.12).

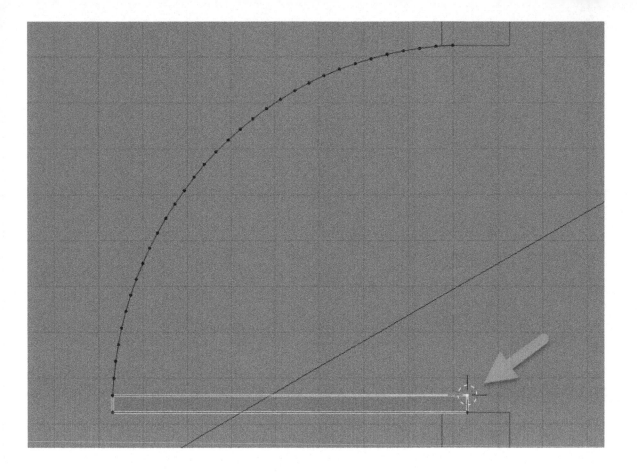

Figure 5.12 - *3D Cursor aligned*

Once you have the 3D Cursor aligned, and assuming you are still using it as the pivot point:

1. Select all edges from the arc. You can hold the ALT key and left-click on any edge to select a sequence

2. Press the E key to extrude

3. Press the ESC key to cancel any transformation

4. Press the S key

5. Type 0 in your keyboard

6. Press RETURN to confirm

With this sequence, you will apply a scale with a size of zero to all of your edges, which will result in a large 3D face for the arc object. Next, you can select the arc edges, and with a right-click add a "Mark Free-Style Edge" (Figure 5.13).

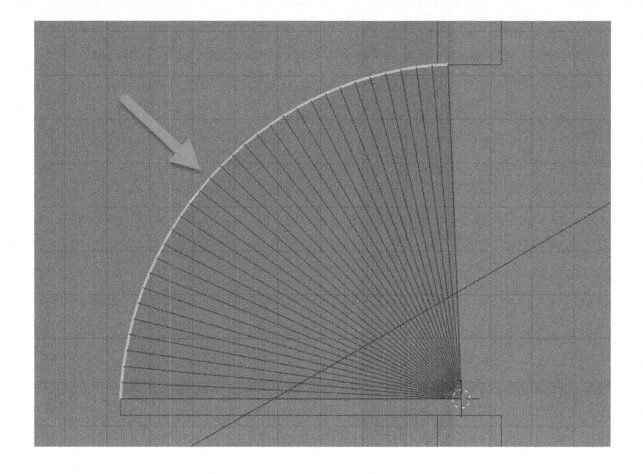

Figure 5.13 - *Arc with edge marks*

Select all the arc object and press the P key to separate it from the door. Choose the Selected option after pressing the P key. Make sure the arc object is in the Viewing Collection. You can also select the door object and press the P key to separate it from the rest of the doors.

If you start a render now, you will see the door with an arc appearing at the floor plan (Figure 5.14).

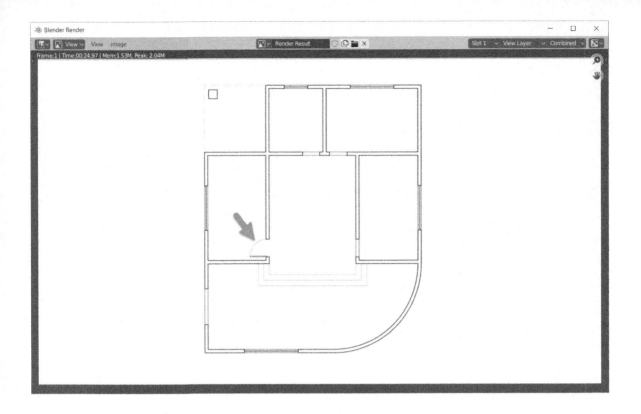

Figure 5.14 - Door with arc

With the first door ready, you can replicate the process in all other doors from the floor plan. Since some doors share the same dimensions, you can easily copy and mirror the door model to save a significant amount of time.

5.3.2 Door and arc origin points

As a way to make your life easier when copying the doors and arcs, you can relocate the origin point of those objects and use the Snap. Once you have the origin point in a location that will help you insert the door, it will be only a matter of aligning the 3D Cursor and move the object.

Where is the best place to align the origin point? Select the same vertex used to rotate the door object. You will find the vertex pointed in Figure 5.9. Align the 3D Cursor with that vertex and select both the door object and arc.

In Object Mode, use the **Object → Set Origin → Origin to 3D Cursor** menu to move your origin point to that location. It will make both objects share the same origin point.

5.3.3 Creating mirrored doors

Since a lot of doors in the floor plan have a similar dimension, and it would be counterproductive to create all of them again, you can duplicate an existing door. However, you will have to apply some rotation to create certain types of doors and also mirror them.

A quick way to create a mirrored version of any object in Blender is by applying a scale with a "-1" value. For instance, you can select both the door and arc and:

1. Press SHIFT+D keys to duplicate

2. Move the copied object away from the original selection

3. Click anywhere to confirm the new location

4. Press the S key

5. Press the X key

6. Type -1

7. Press RETURN to confirm

The sequence will create a mirrored version of your object in the X-axis. You can repeat the same process and replace step 5 with the Y key to creating a vertically mirrored copy.

5.3.4 Aligning doors with the Snap

If you have the origin point of the door object at the right location, it will be extremely easy to place each one of the copies. For instance, if you look at the model shown in Figure 5.15, you will see that we have the 3D cursor at the same location where we would rotate the door object.

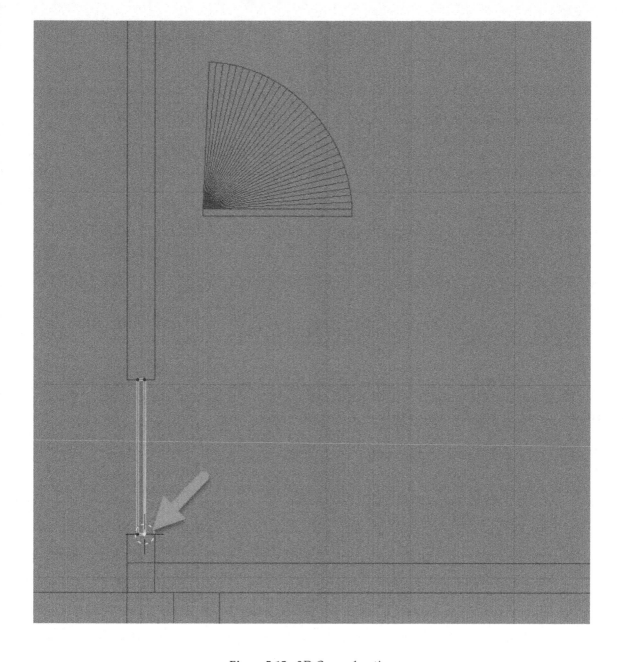

Figure 5.15 - *3D Cursor location*

Instead of creating all the objects for that door, we can use the Snap to quickly move an existing door and arc objects to that location. Select both the door and arc and press the SHIFT+S keys. From the Snap menu, you can choose "Selected to Cursor" (Figure 5.16).

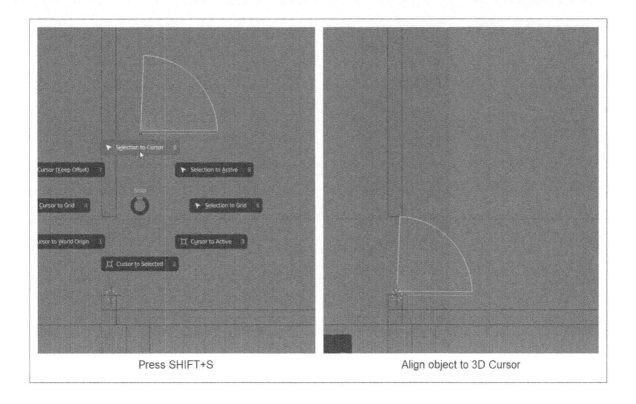

| Press SHIFT+S | Align object to 3D Cursor |

Figure 5.16 - *Moving the door object*

It will make the door and arc to align with the 3D Cursor, and you will quickly have the door objects at the right location. It will only work if you have the origin point located at the base of your door object. After moving the copied door, you can erase any existing model representing the door in a closed state.

Info: *All door objects and arcs are in the Viewing collection.*

5.4 Creating a double-sided door

Some doors in a project require special attention because they have unique features like the large double-sided door at the entrance of our building. To begin with, the unique features a door that at the entrance usually has a small step. We can create that step by marking only the left edge of the door object (Figure 5.17).

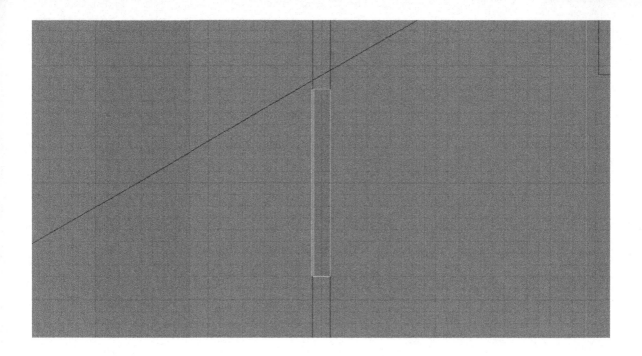

Figure 5.17 - *Door with left edge marked*

Select all edges that you don't want to receive a stroke and with a right-click to choose "Clear FreeStyle Edge."

Next, we can start creating the door objects and arcs for the double-sided door. You will notice that most of the processes will work in a similar way from what we already described in section 5.3.

In Edit Mode, select all vertices from the door object and align the 3D cursor with the vertices. You can use the SHIFT+S key to align the cursor:

1. With the vertices still selected, press the SHIFT+D keys

2. Press the ESC key

3. Make sure you are using the 3D Cursor as the pivot point

4. Press the S key

5. Press the X key

6. Type 0.25

7. Press RETURN to confirm

The sequence will create a smaller version of the door object (Figure 5.18).

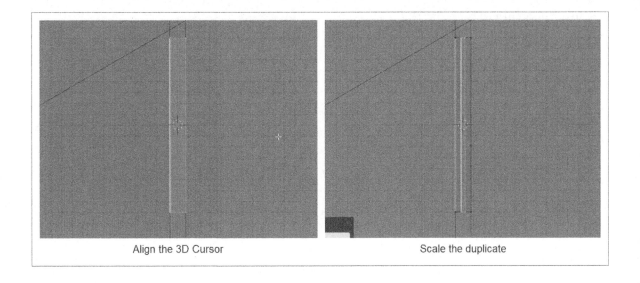

| Align the 3D Cursor | Scale the duplicate |

Figure 5.18 - *Reduced door object*

Using that smaller object as a reference, you can align the 3D cursor with the top-right vertex of that object (Figure 5.19).

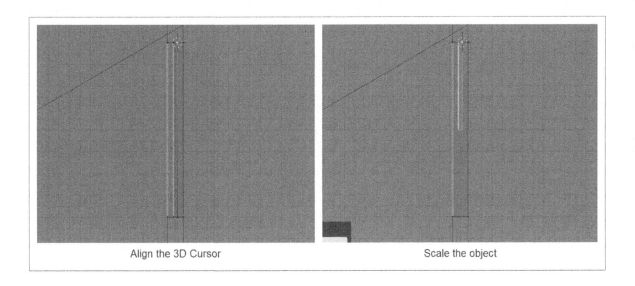

| Align the 3D Cursor | Scale the object |

Figure 5.19 - *Align and scale the door*

To create the object shown in Figure 5.19:

1. Select the vertex

2. Press the SHIFT+S keys

3. Choose "Cursor to Selected"

4. Press CTRL+L to select all connected vertices

5. Press the S key

6. Press the Y key

7. Type 0.5

8. Press RETURN to confirm

The result will be a scale applied to the Y-axis with a factor of 0.5. A scale with that factor will reduce the object size in half. With the vertices still selected:

1. Press the R key

2. Press the Z key

3. Type 90

4. Press RETURN to confirm

You will have the object rotated 90 degrees in the Z-axis (Figure 5.20).

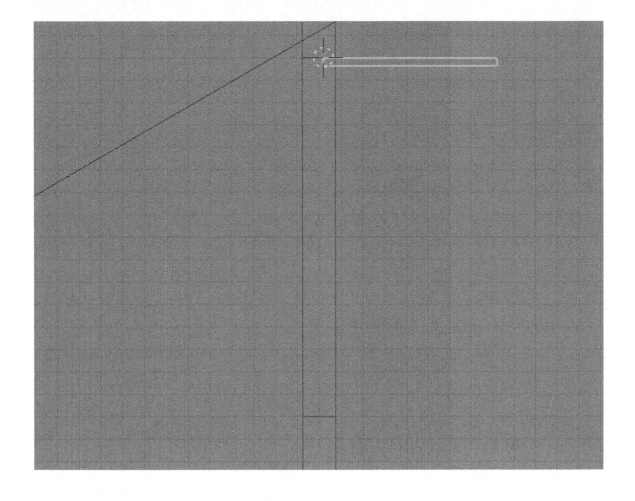

Figure 5.20 - *Rotated door*

Select the vertex indicated in Figure 5.21 and apply a Spin using 85 degrees for angle and 32 Steps (Figure 5.21).

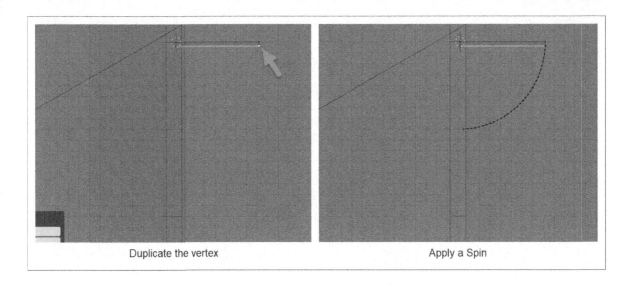

| Duplicate the vertex | Apply a Spin |

Figure 5.21 - Creating the arc

Apply the same technique used earlier to create the faces for the arc. With an extrude that has a size of zero, you can create the arc object (Figure 5.22).

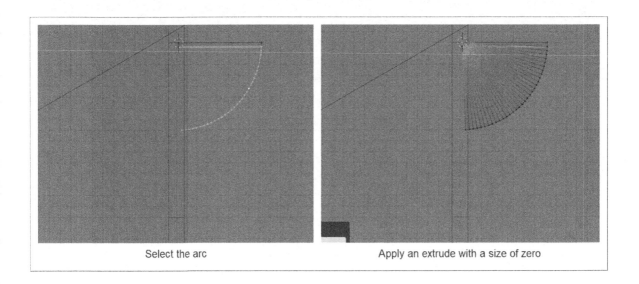

| Select the arc | Apply an extrude with a size of zero |

Figure 5.22 - Creating the faces

As you can see from the previous three Figures, the location of your 3D Cursor should stay at the same location. Select the door object and press the P key to separate it from the doors, and also separate the arc.

Select the edges you wish to use in the technical drawing and apply a FreeStyle Edge (Figure 5.23).

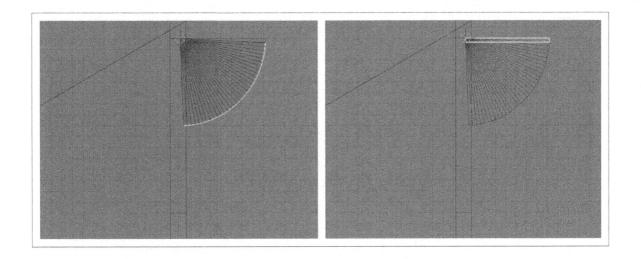

Figure 5.23 - Marking edges

To create a mirrored copy of the door, we will use a different location for the origin point. Select the arc object, and in Edit Mode, you should align the 3D Cursor to the last vertex of the arc. Once you have the 3D Cursor there, you can select both the arc and door objects.

Go to the **Object → Set Origin → Origin to 3D Cursor** menu, and you will have the origin point placed at the end of your arc (Figure 5.24).

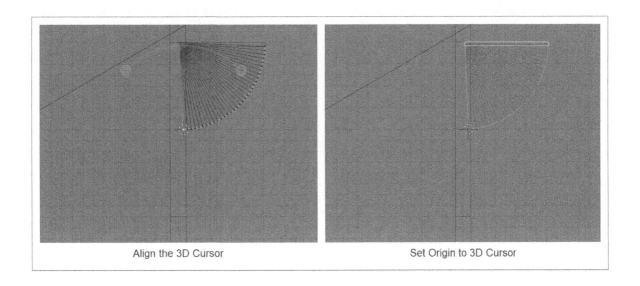

Align the 3D Cursor   Set Origin to 3D Cursor

Figure 5.24 - Origin point

Since you have the origin point at this location, you can quickly create the mirrored version of your door and arc. With both objects selected:

173

1. Press the SHIFT+D keys

2. Press the ESC key

3. Press the S key

4. Press the Y key

5. Type -1

6. Press RETURN to confirm

It will create a mirrored copy of your door and arc (Figure 5.25).

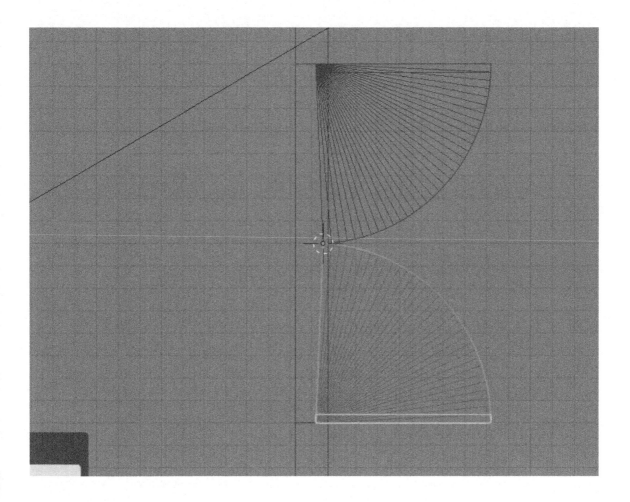

Figure 5.25 - *Mirrored copy*

If you render the floor plan after adding and adjusting all the doors and arcs, you will have a much better representation of a technical drawing (Figure 5.26).

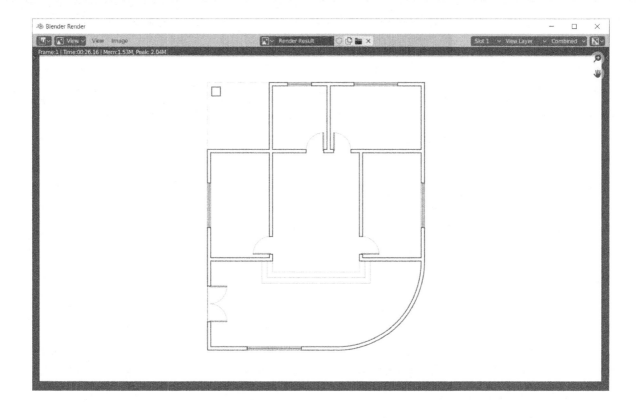

Figure 5.26 - *Floor plan with all doors*

Regarding a floor plan, you can also use a straight line instead of an arc to represent doors, which will make the process a lot easier. You can create a triangular shape to represent the line and mark only one edge to render.

5.5 Importing CAD blocks

A common element from any technical drawing is the use of an asset called block. Those blocks usually have furniture and other elements that help to give a sense of scale and add context to the drawing. A quick search online will show you a wide variety of blocks available in formats like DWG and DXF.

In Blender, you can easily import DXF files to your projects and prepare them to render with FreeStyle, but working with DWG files is a challenge in any platform. What would be the process to import a block to our floor plan? In the following sections, we will get a file in DWG format and convert it to DXF.

That way, it will be possible to use standard Blender tools to import and adjust the block to the drawing. The block we will use is a desk with some chairs for the reception space.

5.5.1 Converting DWG to DXF

If you get a block that is in DWG format, you won't be able to import it directly to Blender unless converted to a more friendly format like DXF. Luckily for us, you will find a great and free tool called ODA File Converter that can transform almost any version of DWG files to DXF.

To download the ODA File Converter, you must visit the following link:

`https://www.opendesign.com/guestfiles/oda_file_converter`

There you will find multiple versions of the converter for systems like:

- Windows

- macOS

- Linux

The converter works only in batch mode, where you will have to create an Input and Output folders. Place the DWG files in the Input folder, and select the version you wish to use for your DXF files. Press the Start button to begin converting the files. If you want to ensure compatibility with Blender, a version like 2010 ASCII DXF will work great.

5.5.2 Importing DXF files to Blender

Once you have the block saved as a DXF file, it is time to import it to Blender. If you open the **File → Import** menu, you won't see any option there to import DXF files by default. That is because you must enable an Add-on that will help to import DXF files.

Go to the **Edit → Preferences** menu, and at the Add-ons tab, you can type "DXF" at the search box, and you will see all options related to DXF files. Enable the Add-on that enables you to import DXF files (Figure 5.27).

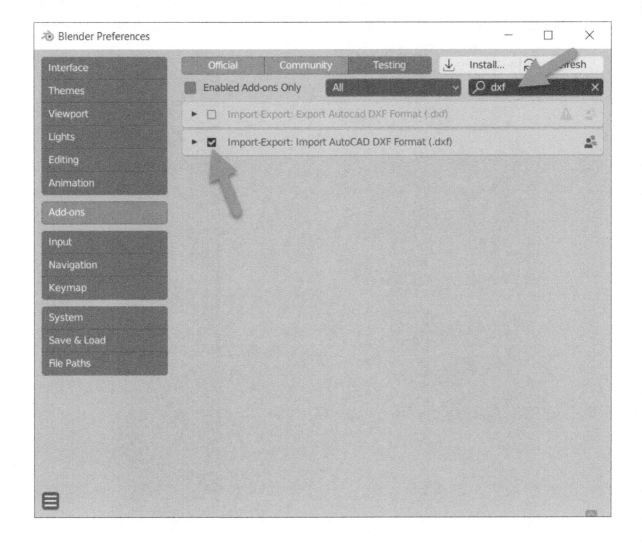

Figure 5.27 - Enabling the Add-on

After enabling the Add-on, you will start to see an option to import DXF files at the **File → Import** menu (Figure 5.28).

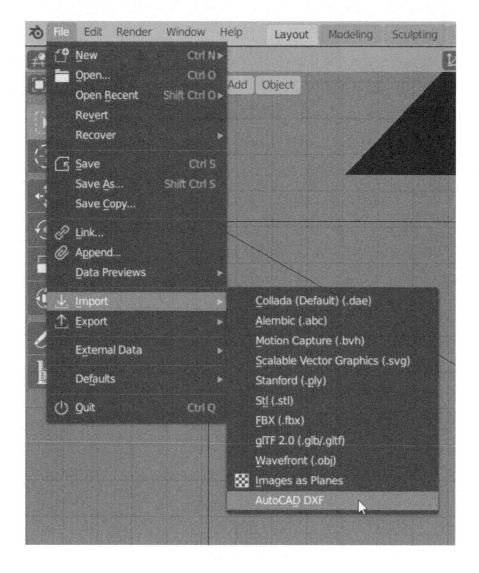

Figure 5.28 - Importing DXF from the File menu

When you choose the AutoCAD DXF option, you will see the Blender file selector, where you can locate and import the DXF file.

5.5.3 Cleaning DXF blocks

When importing DXF blocks to Blender, you will most likely have to perform form cleanup in the drawing to use in a technical drawing render. Those drawings will usually present several problems that need a fix. For instance, most of them will appear in Blender as a Curve and not a Mesh object.

One of the first steps in the cleanup process is to convert any block coming from a DXF file to Mesh. You can do that by selecting the block, and in Object Mode, use the **Object → Convert to → Mesh from**

Curve/Meta/Text menu. That will create a Mesh object that we can edit and add features like 3D planes and FreeStyle Edges.

In Figure 5.29, you can see the block imported from a DXF file, and that has a Mesh format.

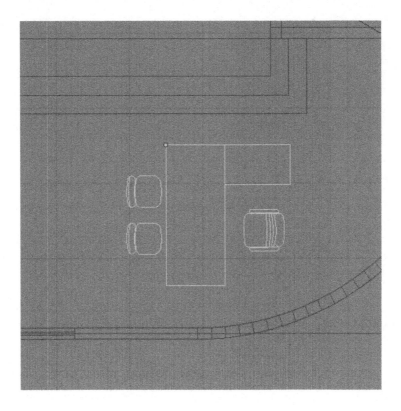

Figure 5.29 - Block with desk and chairs

It looks like a regular drawing that would appear in a render, but it has a major problem. If you remember the simple rule about FreeStyle, which states that you must have a 3D face to add strokes, an object that has only edges will not appear in a render.

The desk block doesn't have any 3D faces, and we will have to add them to the drawing manually. To add a face, you can select a group of vertices that form a shape and press the F key. However, in some cases, you will still don't have a 3D face.

A few parts of the model will only generate a face after you merge them into a single object. For instance, in Figure 5.30, you can see a separated group of vertices from the chair.

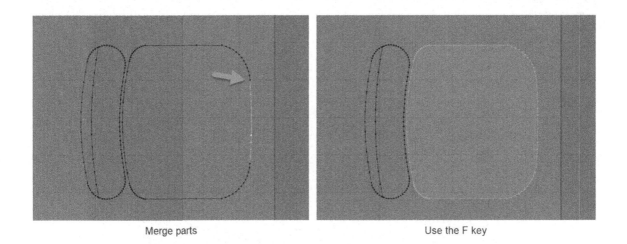

Merge parts   Use the F key

Figure 5.30 - *Separated vertices*

Those vertices will prevent the creation of a 3D face for FreeStyle in the chair block. But, if you select the two vertices at the edge of each separate part (with the B key) and with the right mouse button, open the Context Menu. There you can use the Merge → By Distance to connect both vertices.

Repeat the same procedure for the vertices at the bottom, and you will be able to create a 3D face with the F key. Each furniture model will require a unique workflow for editing and demand some investigation to find loose vertices and missing parts.

If you manage to add all 3D faces to the objects, move the block to the Viewing Collection with the M key and add the "Mark FreeStyle Edge" to all edges you want to appear in the render (Figure 5.31).

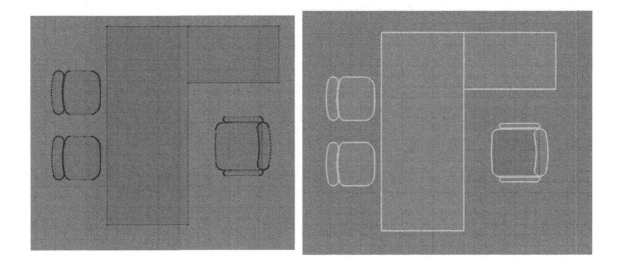

Figure 5.31 - Block with edge marks

A render will show the block with all the strokes necessary for a technical drawing render (Figure 5.32).

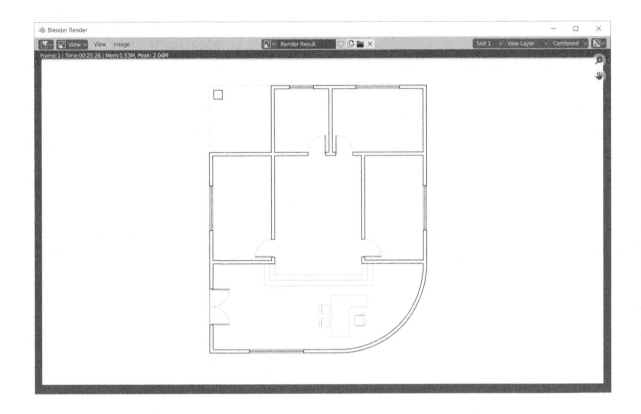

Figure 5.32 - Render with furniture block

Since the editing and processing of furniture models can take some time in Blender, a great way to optimize future projects is saving those blocks in a Blender file. Later you will be able to Append them to a new technical drawing with all the 3D faces and marks ready for rendering.

What is next?

When you make some of the tasks described in this chapter, you will notice that it requires a lot of manual work to set up elements such as doors and windows. That is the impression after working on a floor plan for the first time. If you have plans to keep working with such elements in Blender and making more technical drawings, you should consider making each element an asset.

After you set up a door or window, you can rename the object with something that will identify the element. For instance, select a window and press the F2 key. Assign a name like "Window80," and you will be able to identify that it represents a window with 0.80 units quickly.

Save that file in your hard drive or local network for future use. Every time you have to make a new floor plan, it will be possible to get those assets for reuse. In the **File → Append** menu, you can select any existing Blender file and "import" any object to the current project.

If you keep the habit of saving the elements you create for each project, after a couple of drawings, you will start to have a library of assets to use in future projects. Start saving assets for technical drawing! That is your next step.

Chapter 6 - View Layers and annotations

When you start to create objects for a technical drawing that must render without the settings from Free-Style, you will face a problem. The settings for FreeStyle in the render disables the visualization of surfaces. That will be a problem for elements such as text.

If you render the project using settings from FreeStyle, all objects will appear with an outline and no solid color. Regardless of materials and shapes, you will only get an outline. What if you want to render shaded objects mixed with a technical drawing?

That is when Blender View Layers will become incredibly useful, and you will learn how to use View Layers to create unique visuals for your technical drawings. We will use it to add text and later include some commonly used symbols for technical drawing.

Here is a list of what you will learn:

- Adding annotations for technical drawing

- Materials for annotations

- Working with View Layers

- Composing View Layers

- Replicating annotations

- Disabling composing for rendering

6.1 Adding annotations for technical drawing

A technical drawing requires a significant amount of information to appear, and sometimes, you will need annotations to explain the purpose of a project. If you look to a floor plan, you will probably identify what a wall or door is, but the purpose of a room requires a label. In Blender, we can add text objects that will help with the creation of such labels.

To create a text object in Blender, you can press SHIFT+A in Object Mode and choose the Text option. A text in Blender is a unique type of object that has properties such as:

- Fonts

- Size

- Alignment

Before you start adding any text objects to the floor plan, you should first create a new Collection called Text to organize the project (Figure 6.1).

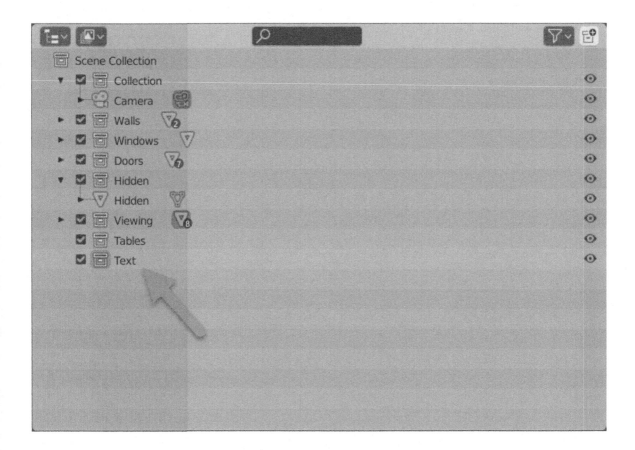

Figure 6.1 - *Collection for text*

If you already have any text objects in the project, you can use the M key to move any one of those objects to the Text Collection. Later we will configure a Line Set for the Collection.

You will be able to manipulate a text object in Blender like any other 3D model. All transformation shortcuts and like the G, R, and S keys will work. To edit the contents of your text object, you will use Edit Mode. By selecting the text object and going to Edit Mode, you can change the text by typing.

For instance, we can select the text object and use the TAB key to use Edit Mode. There you can hit the BACKSPACE key or DELETE key to erase the default text. Type "Reception" for the text, and we will have that as the new 3D text (Figure 6.2).

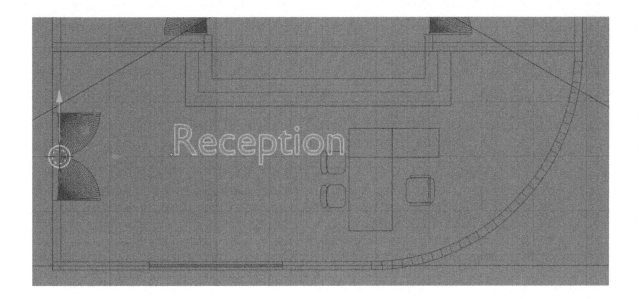

Figure 6.2 - *3D Text in the floor plan*

After changing the text contents, you can easily relocate and place the text object anywhere you want at the floor plan. Use the R key to change rotation and sizes with the S key. However, we can also set the size in the Object Data Properties.

6.1.1 Text properties and font

When you select a text object in Blender, all options from the Object Data Properties will change to display options to customize the text. There you can change aspects of the text such as font, size, and alignment. You can see some of those properties in Figure 6.3.

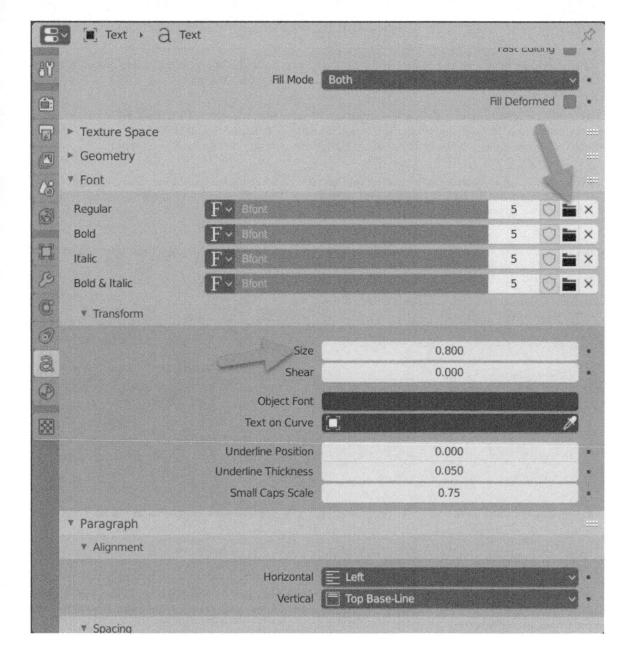

Figure 6.3 - Text properties

For instance, at the Font group, you can pick a unique font file from your system to use in Blender. Click at the folder button to open a font from your system (Figure 6.4).

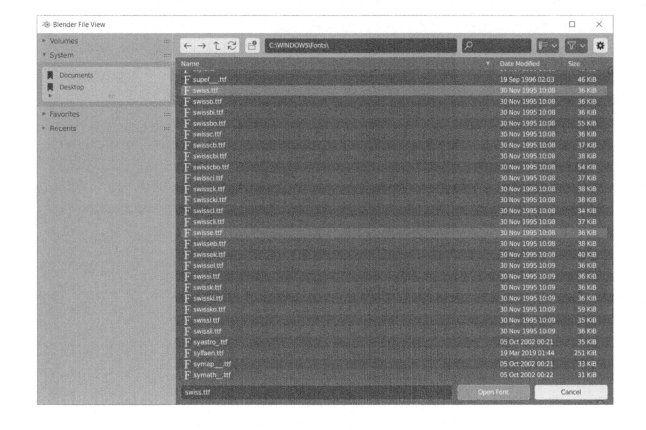

Figure 6.4 - Selecting a font

You can choose a font for different text styles, such as regular, bold, and italic. Below the options to choose a font, you can also change the text size.

Tip: Change all settings from your text object and make copies of the object with the SHIFT+D keys. That will help you keep the same style for all texts in the technical drawing.

6.2 Materials for annotations

The floor plan we are creating has all the strokes rendered with black color in a white background. To match the same visual style, we have to use all text objects with black color. To have all text objects with black color, we have to apply a material to the object. Select the text and go to the Properties Editor.

There you will open the Material Properties tab to see all options related to materials (Figure 6.5).

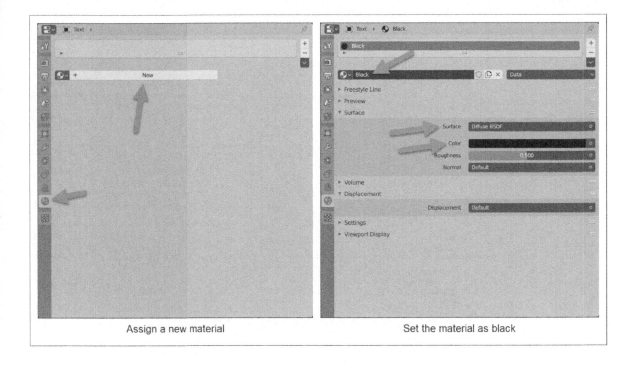

| Assign a new material | Set the material as black |

Figure 6.5 - Adding a material

Since we created a new object, you will probably have to add new material to the text. You will see an empty list of options with only a button "New" available. After hitting the "New" button, you will see a lot of options to edit your material.

At the top, you can start by renaming the material to "black" and also the "Surface" option to "Diffuse BSDF." The material will usually start with "Surface" using "Principled BSDF," but we can use a much simpler alternative for the text.

Below the "Surface" option, you will see "Color" that will let you pick a pitch-black color for the material.

6.3 Working with View Layers

After adding the materials to the text, we can prepare for a render to see how the text object will appear in the floor plan. Before rendering the project, you can create a new Line Set for the text object and make it render only the Collection called Text. Assign the same Line Style used for the Viewing Line Set.

In our case, you should use the Line Style "ContinousLine-1.0" to render that Line Set. If you hit the F12 key to start a render, you will see the text (Figure 6.6).

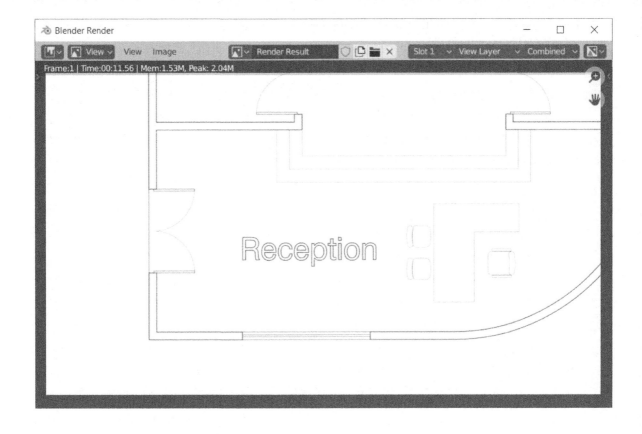

Figure 6.6 - Text at the floor plan

Using the current settings, the text will appear in the floor plan with only an outline. What if we wanted the text to have a solid fill?

If you want the text to render with a solid fill color, we must use a feature of Blender called View Layer. The reason to use such a feature is that we must find a way to disable the Filter settings for the text-only. Back in chapter 2, we learned about an option available only in Cycles that will let us disable the render of surfaces.

Since we are using the Filter option to render only the lines in a technical drawing, it is also disabling any surfaces from the text. To have a text with a solid fill, you need the "Surface" option enabled.

That is where a View Layer will help us create unique settings and separate the text from all other drawing elements.

6.3.1 Creating new View Layers

The View Layers in Blender plays a major role in projects that require unique settings to render objects like a technical drawing. Because you can mix and blend different settings to render an object using FreeStyle and others that have a traditional shading.

Where are the View Layers? In the Blender user interface, you see a View Layer selector at the top right corner of your screen (Figure 6.7).

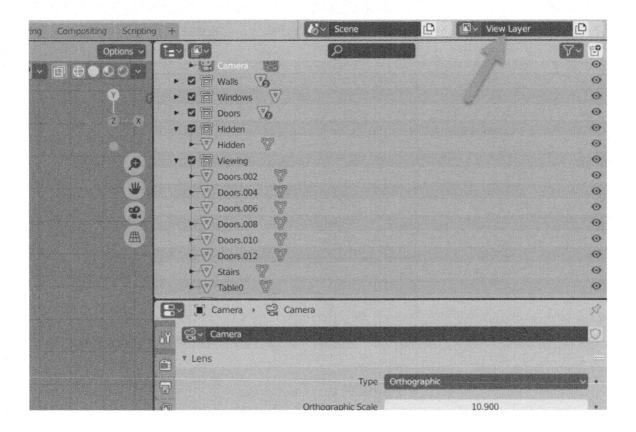

Figure 6.7 - View Layer selector

A project will always start with at least one View Layer that uses Collections to control how everything appears in a render. It is possible to rename a View Layer by clicking at the current name to erase and set a new name.

Rename the existing View Layer of our floor plan to "Drawing" that will control all graphical elements of the project. You can create a new View Layer by clicking at the button on the right of your View Layer name (Figure 6.8).

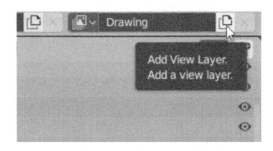

Figure 6.8 - *New View Layer*

Assign the name "Text" to the new View Layer to control all text objects. You can easily change the active View Layer using the button on the left of your View Layer name.

With the Text View Layer selected, open the View Layer Properties to see what makes View Layers in Blender special. There you won't see any of the Line Sets from the floor plan (Figure 6.9).

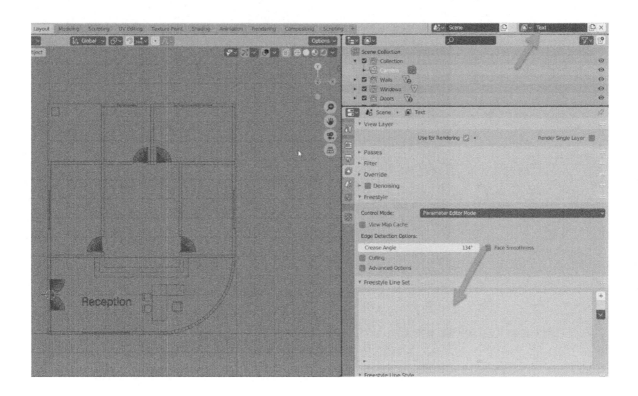

Figure 6.9 - *View Layer Properties*

If you render the floor plan now with the Text View Layer selected, you won't see any of the FreeStyle strokes. Each View Layer can have unique settings for rendering.

Tip: *You can have as many View Layers as you need in a project. To render a mix of those View Layers, we will have to use the Composite Editor of Blender.*

6.3.2 View Layers for technical drawing

Since each View Layer can accept unique settings for rendering, we can set up both of the existing View Layers to work differently. The View Layer called "Drawing" will keep all the settings from FreeStyle with Line Sets and also the Filter option with Surfaces disabled.

The new View Layer called "Text" doesn't have any Line Sets and will have the Surface option enabled. If you want to ensure that it doesn't render any strokes, you can also disable "FreeStyle" from the Filter options.

In Figure 6.10, you will see both the View Layer settings side by side.

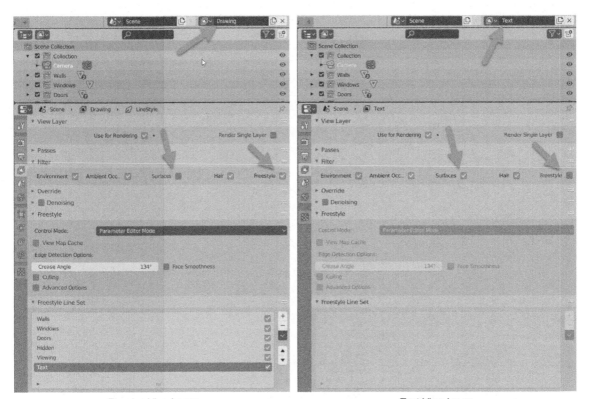

Drawing View Layer   Text View Layer

Figure 6.10 - *View Layer Settings for technical drawing*

Use the selector at the top right to change the current View Layer and make all necessary adjustments to the settings.

6.3.3 View Layers and Collections

Having multiple View Layers will help to organize the project for rendering, but Blender still doesn't know what objects to render in each View Layer. Each View Layer will use all enabled Collections for rendering when you press the F12 key. That means you can remove objects from a View Layer by disabling a Collection from the currently selected View Layer.

For instance, if you choose the View Layer "Text" and disable all Collections but the "Text," you have that View Layer rendering the objects on that Collection only (Figure 6.11).

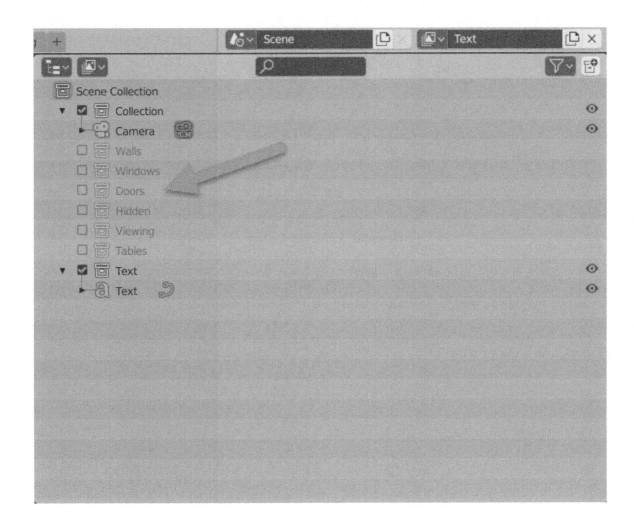

Figure 6.11 *- View Layer and Collections*

To disable a Collection from a View Layer, you can click at the checkbox on the left of each Collection or press the E key at the Outliner Editor. Select the Collection name and press E to disable and ALT+E to enable it again.

In our case, you will make the View Layer "Text" to have only the "Text" Collection enabled. The View Layer "Drawing" has the opposite settings with the "Text" Collection disabled and all others enabled (Figure 6.12).

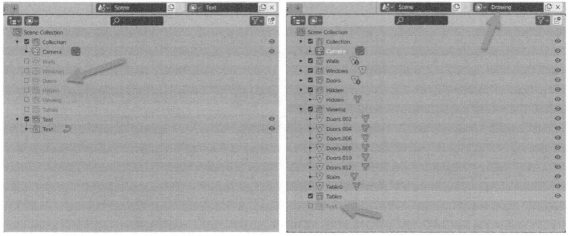

Text View Layer   Drawing View Layer

Figure 6.12 - *Collection settings*

Once you disable the Text Collection with the View Layer Drawing, you will no longer see the text objects in your floor plan. To avoid having to swap between two View Layers, you can enable the Collection for editing and manipulating the text and disable that when before rendering.

At the Render Properties tab, we can enable an option called Transparent to remove the background from all renders (Figure 6.13).

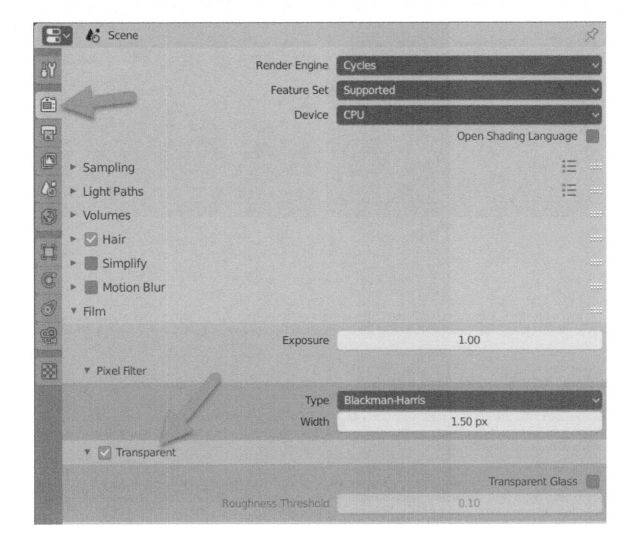

Figure 6.13 - *Transparent option*

If you render the floor plan now, you will see the text object with a black fill color because it is already using the settings from the "Text" View Layer (Figure 6.14).

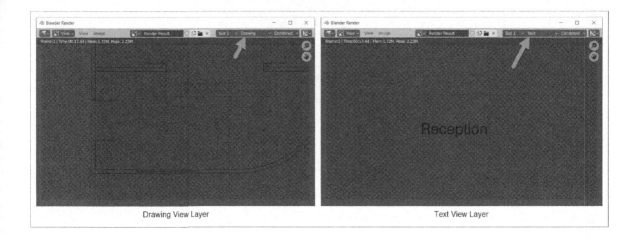

Drawing View Layer   Text View Layer

Figure 6.14 - *Render with View Layers*

When using View Layers, you will have two images as the output. At the top of your render window, it is possible to change the View Layer you want to see from the output window.

6.4 Composing View Layers

As you could see from Figure 6.13, a render using View Layers will produce separate results that we must compose to have a unique image. In Blender, we have an editor called Compositor that will help mix the results of multiple View Layers.

At the top of your user interface, you will see a tab called "Composition" that will display a user interface arrangement with that editor. Click on that tab to see your user interface change to use the Compositor Editor (Figure 6.15).

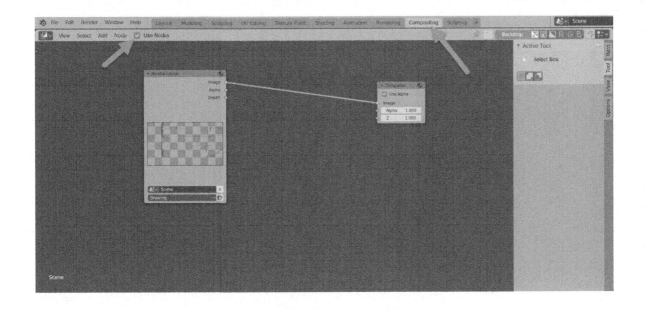

Figure 6.15 - *Compositor Editor*

At the top of the Compositor Editor, you can enable "Use Nodes" to start seeing the Nodes. There will be one Node called "Render Layers" and another one "Composite."

A few important points about Nodes:

– Inside the Composite Editor, you will be able to use all shortcuts for selection, object manipulation, and zoom

– You can create new Nodes with the SHIFT+A key or the Add menu

– Each Node can have either input or output sockets

– The sockets are the small circles on at each side

– On the left, you have input sockets, and the ones on the right are output sockets

– The sockets have a color code to identify data types. You should connect sockets with the same color

– To connect sockets, you can click and drag from one socket to the other with the left mouse button

– You can cut a connection by holding the CTRL key while clicking and dragging with the right mouse button. The cursor will turn to a knife that can cut connection lines

You can start the composition process for our technical drawing render by selecting the existing Render Layers Node and press the SHIFT+D keys to make a copy. With the copied Render Layers, you can change the current View Layer to "Text" at the bottom (Figure 6.16).

197

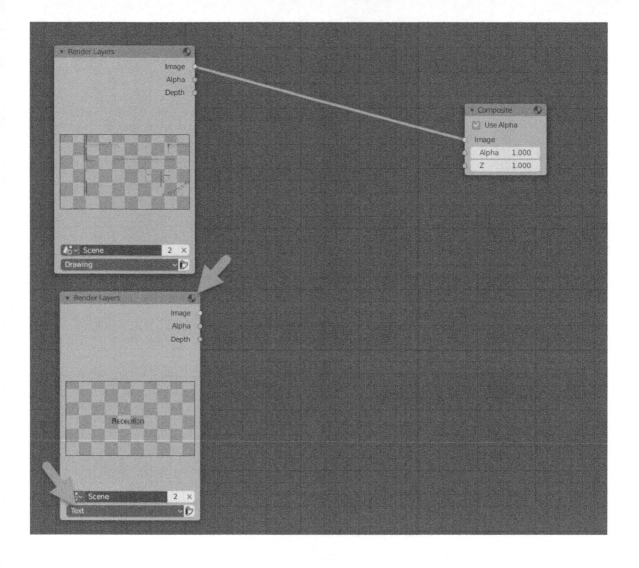

Figure 6.16 - *New Render Layer Node*

Press the SHIFT+A keys, and from the Color group, you can add a Node called Alpha Over (Figure 6.17).

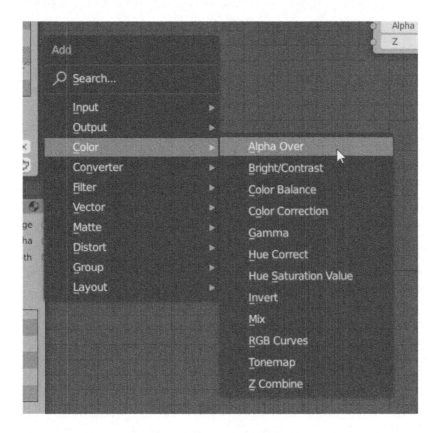

Figure 6.17 - *Alpha Over Node*

The Node will help us mixing the results of two View Layers and output them as a single image. Break the current connection of the Render Layer with the "Drawing" View Layer to the Composite Node.

Now, we can rearrange the connections:

1. From the Render Layers Node with the "Drawing" View Layer, you will connect the Image output socket to the top Image input socket of your Alpha Over.

2. From the Render Layers Node with the "Text" View Layer, you will connect the Image output socket to the bottom Image input socket of your Alpha Over.

3. From the Alpha Over Node, you will connect the Image output socket to the Composite Node Image input socket.

The Node arrangement will look like Figure 6.18 shows.

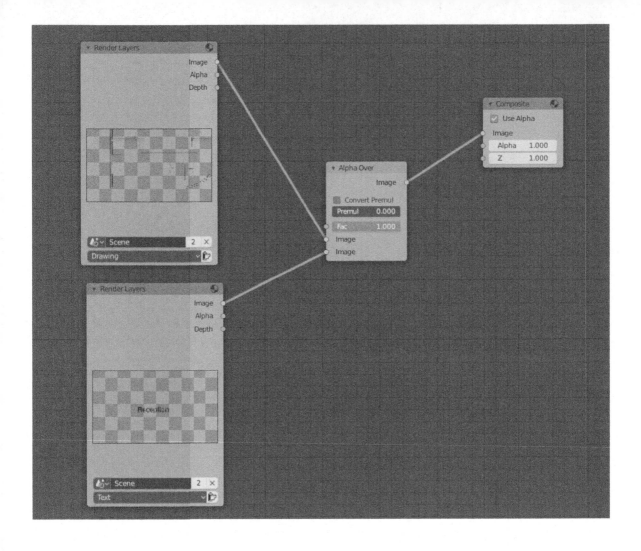

Figure 6.18 - *Nodes for technical drawing*

If you press the F12 key now to start a render, you will see the two View Layers in a single render (Figure 6.19).

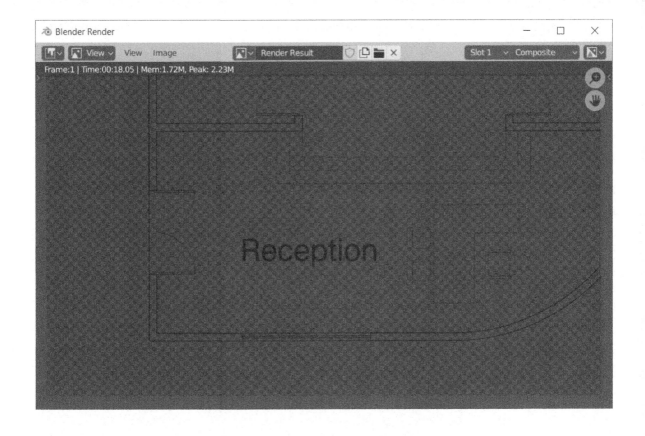

Figure 6.19 - *Render results from composition*

You can control the order used to display each View Layer in a render with the Alpha Over Node. The Render Layers connected to the top Image input socket will appear at the back. Anyone connected to the bottom Image input socket will render at the front.

Tip: At any moment, you can exit the Compositing WorkSpace and go back to the Layout. Use the tabs at the top of your user interface to change the editors in the interface.

6.4.1 Adding a white background

The results we are getting from the render using the Composing have a transparent background because that is necessary to blend both View Layers. What if we wanted the white background back? To have a white background from the Compositing, we will have to add another Alpha Over Node.

Select the existing Alpha Over Node and press the SHIFT+D keys. Place the new Node on the right of your existing Alpha Over Node. When you don't use any Render Layer as input for a socket in the Alpha Over Node, it is possible to choose a fill color.

The top Image input socket from the Alpha Over Node controls the images at the bottom of your renders. With that in mind, we can break the existing connection from the first Alpha Over Node to the Composite Node. Connect the first Alpha Over to the bottom Image input socket of the second Alpha Over Node.

Make sure you have a white color in the top image field for the second Alpha Over Node. Connect that Node to the Composite Node (Figure 6.20).

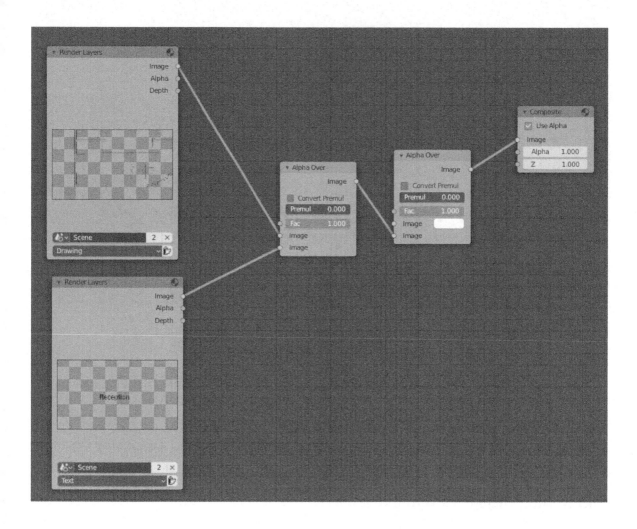

Figure 6.20 - *Nodes for white background*

If you press the F12 key now to render the project, you should see a white background for the floor plan again (Figure 6.21).

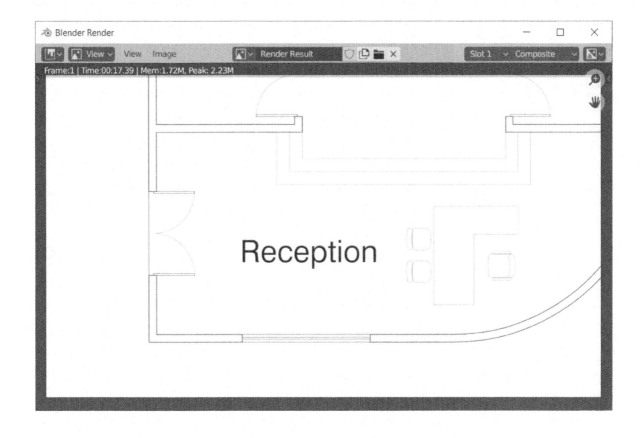

Figure 6.21 - *Floor plan with a white background*

The Compositing options are a powerful way to mix and blend View Layers to create unique settings and effects for technical drawing in Blender. For instance, you can create settings to add 3D models that have materials and shading from Cycles and mix them with a technical drawing.

Using View Layers and the Compositing options, it is possible to create unique presentations and visuals for technical drawing.

6.5 Replicating annotations

After you have the text object rendering with a black fill color and two View Layers to control how each Collection appears at the Render, it is time to add all other text labels to the floor plan. To help you align and view each text object, you can choose the "Drawing" View Layer and enable the "Text" Collection.

Select the text object, and with the SHIFT+D keys, duplicate the text five times. Each new label will go to a room of the floor plan. Using the TAB key with a text selected, you can edit the contents of each object. In our case, we are using the following labels shown in Figure 6.22.

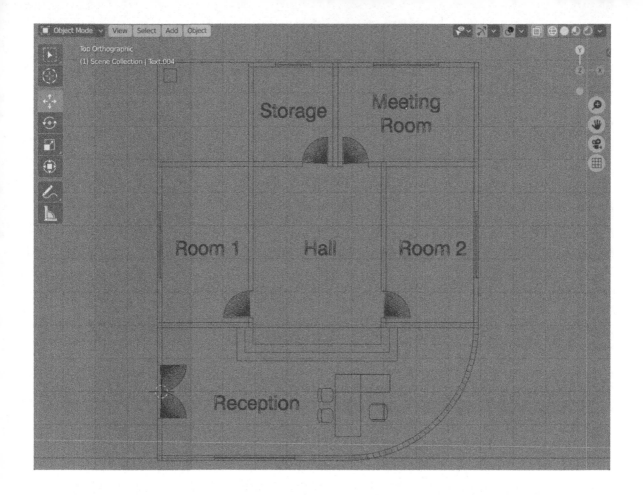

Figure 6.22 - *Floor plan with text objects*

To align and place each text object in a room, you will have to use either the transform widget or G key. After you have all text object in Blender, you can disable the "Text" Collection for rendering. Select that Collection from the Outliner Editor and press the E key.

If you don't disable the Collection, it will appear in the render with an outline for all text objects.

Tip: You don't have to add materials to the new text objects because we are copying an object that already has the black material. If you choose to create new objects with the SHIFT+A key, you will have to add new materials to them.

6.5.1 Text alignment

From Figure 6.22, you will notice that one of the text labels has two words with a centralized alignment. To align a text object that has multiple parts, you must use the options from the Object Data Properties. Select the text and open those properties (Figure 6.23).

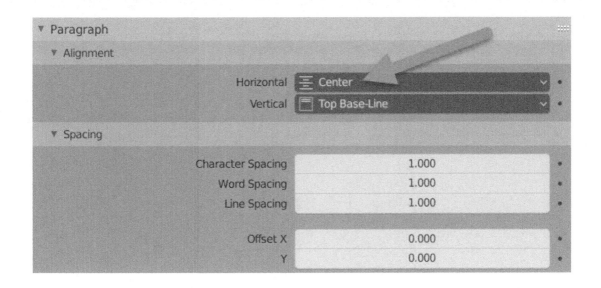

Figure 6.23 - *Text options*

There you will find a field that has all the options to edit a paragraph. Change the horizontal alignment to the Center, and you will have centralized text with multiple lines.

6.6 Disabling composing for rendering

Once you start using the Compositing options in Blender to render projects, you will notice something unique about the project. No matter what you do in the render options, you will always see the results from the Compositing (Figure 6.24).

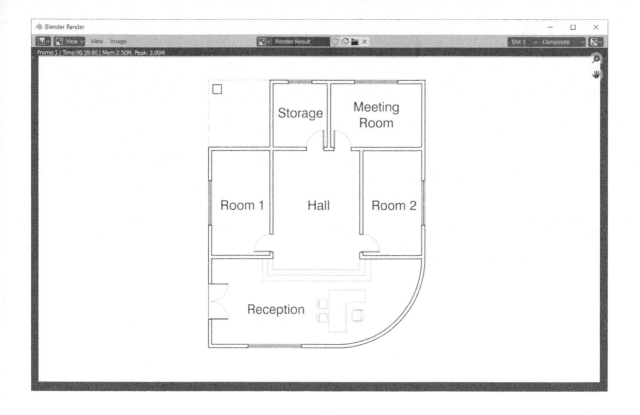

Figure 6.24 - *Composition results*

By default, you will have the results from the Compositing Editor overriding any settings used to render a project in Blender. If you don't want to use the results from your Composing Editor, you will find the settings for that at the Output Properties tab (Figure 6.25).

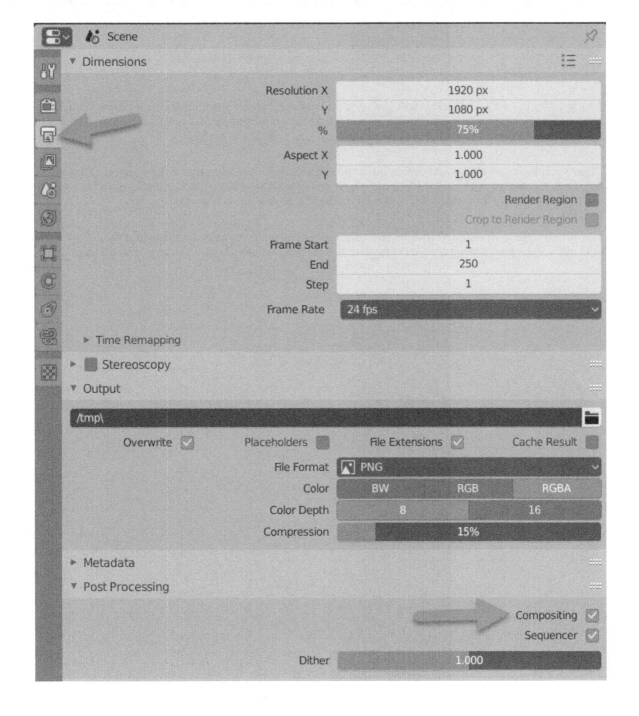

Figure 6.25 - *Output Properties settings*

At the Post Processing options, you can disable the "Compositing" field. After disabling that option, you will see separate View Layers in the Render window.

What is next?

The use of View Layers in Blender will give you all kinds of creative possibilities for a project, which you can use to make compositions and also add new effects for your floor plans. For instance, using a separate View Layer for a floor plan will allow you to create an effect called the poché line.

Have you ever saw a technical drawing that has an area from a section cut or floor plan that has all the parts from the section with a solid black fill? The name of such an effect is poché (poché walls) in architecture, and you can use it for walls and also the ground line, in case of section cuts.

As an exercise to develop your skills and using View Layers, even more, you can add that effect to the walls in the floor plan. Create another version of the drawing where all the walls receive solid fills.

Chapter 7 - Dimension lines and symbols

One of the most tedious parts of any technical drawing is the creation and setup of dimension lines for many artists and professionals. You will have to find all the places and locations in a project that need a dimension line. In Blender, we don't have any tool that will help us adding those lines automatically. At least, with technical drawing rendering in mind.

Unfortunately, you will have to create them manually using that will render like a dimension line. In this chapter, you will learn how to create and setup that type of object and add the text information with the respective dimensions for each line.

Besides a dimension line, you will also learn how to create a common symbol for a floor plan, which is the level symbol.

Here is a list of what you will learn:

- – Creating a dimension line

- – Expanding dimension lines with the Snap

- – Creating internal dimension lines

- – Adding text to dimension lines

- – Creating architectural symbols

7.1 Creating a dimension line

A key feature from any technical drawing involves the presentation of lengths and dimensions. That feature will appear as a dimension line in a technical drawing, which is a line that has special visual markings showing the distance between two locations of a drawing. In Blender, we don't have any dedicated tool or feature that will create dimension lines for technical drawing.

To render a technical drawing with FreeStyle, we have to create all necessary dimension lines manually. Once you create the first one, it will be incredibly easy to replicate the process and make all other dimension lines.

The design of a dimension line for technical drawing in Blender to render with FreeStyle will start with a 3D plane. You can create a plane and using the S key apply a scale to make it look like a rectangle:

1. Press the SHIFT+A keys

2. From the Mesh group create a Plane

3. Press the S key

4. Press the Y key

5. Type 2

6. Press RETURN to confirm

7. Press the S key

8. Press the Y key

9. Type 0.5

10. Press RETURN to confirm

The objective has a rectangle that looks like Figure 7.1 shows.

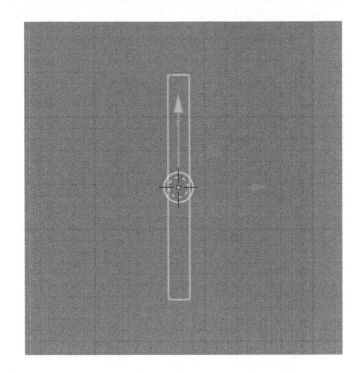

Figure 7.1 - Rectangle to start a dimension line

After you create the object, press the M key, and choose Viewing to make it stay at that Collection (Figure 7.2).

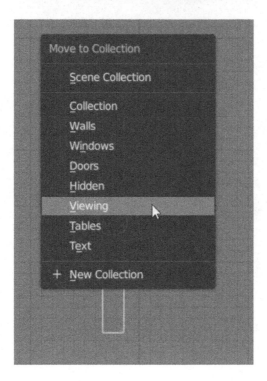

Figure 7.2 - *Move to the Viewing Collection*

A dimension line in a technical drawing usually has a much thinner line thickness than all other lines, which makes the Viewing Collection perfect for that drawing element. You could also create a unique Collection and Line Set for the dimension lines.

The next step is to add a line at the middle of our rectangle using a tool from Blender called Loop Cut:

1. Select the rectangle

2. Press the TAB key to enter Edit Mode

3. Press the CTRL+R keys to start a Loop Cut

4. Place the mouse cursor above the rectangle top edge

5. When you see a vertical yellow line click once with the left mouse button

6. Press the ESC key to maintain the cut at the middle of your rectangle

As a result, you will have a vertical edge that is at the exact middle of your rectangle object (Figure 7.3).

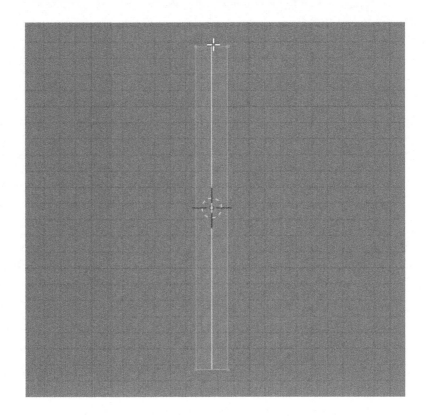

Figure 7.3 - Rectangle with vertical line

The main purpose of that vertical line is to receive a "Mark FreeStyle Edge" later and draw the main stroke for a dimension line.

7.1.1 Adding Edge Marks

The next step to complete the main design for our dimension line is to select all edges that must receive a "Mark FreeStyle Edge." Since we are using the Viewing Collection that has a Line Set with settings to only render strokes for objects that have such mark, it is necessary to set up the edges.

In Edit Mode, you can select the top and bottom edges and also the one in the exact middle (Figure 7.4).

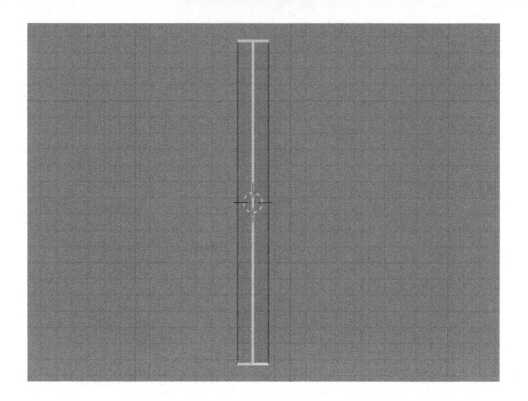

Figure 7.4 - *Selected edges*

Once you have the edges selected, use the right mouse button, then open the context menu and choose "Mark FreeStyle Edge" to add the marking. You can test the design of our dimension line by pressing the F12 key to render (Figure 7.5).

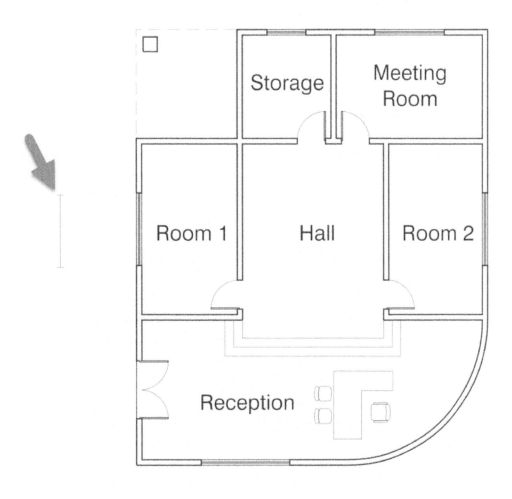

Figure 7.5 - *Dimension line design*

The dimension line design is simple, but you can create other types using the same principles from what we already know from FreeStyle.

7.2 Expanding dimension lines with the Snap

Once you have the first dimension line object ready, it will be easy to expand and make all the other objects. A key tool to place and align dimension lines in Blender is the Snap During Transform because we can easily capture vertices from parts of our floor plan or any other technical drawing.

You must enable the Snap During Transform and choose Vertex as the Snap Element, as we used in previous chapters. Select the dimension line object and go to Edit Mode:

1. Make sure you have the selection mode set to Vertex

2. Press the B key and draw a box around the three vertices on the top or bottom of your dimension line

3. Press the G key

4. Press the Y key (That will be the key for vertical dimension lines)

5. Move the mouse cursor above a vertex of your floor plan until you see the small circle from the Snap

6. Left-click where you want to place the dimension line

Using the Snap During Transform, you can quickly capture points in the floor plan that you can use as a reference (Figure 7.6).

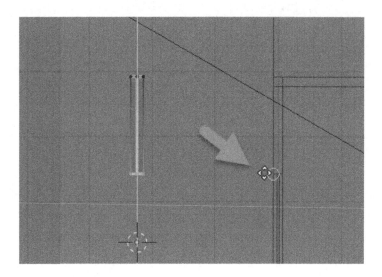

Figure 7.6 - Capturing points for dimension lines

That will work for a small segment of a dimension line, but we can reproduce the same procedure to create a much larger line. Keep the same three vertices selected from either the bottom or top of your line and use an extrude to expand the line.

With the extrude limited to a single axis and the Snap During Transform, you can create all the segments necessary for the dimension line on the left side of our floor plan:

1. Make sure you are in Edit Mode and with the selection mode set to Vertex

2. Keep the Snap During Transform enabled with the element set to Vertex

3. Select the three top or bottom vertices of a dimension line

4. Press the E key to extrude

5. Press the Y key

6. Move the mouse over your floor plan to capture points

7. Left-click to place the dimension line aligned with a vertex

8. Repeat steps 4-7 until you have all the segments from your dimension line

If you follow those steps to create a dimension line sequence of extrudes, you will get a much larger object (Figure 7.7).

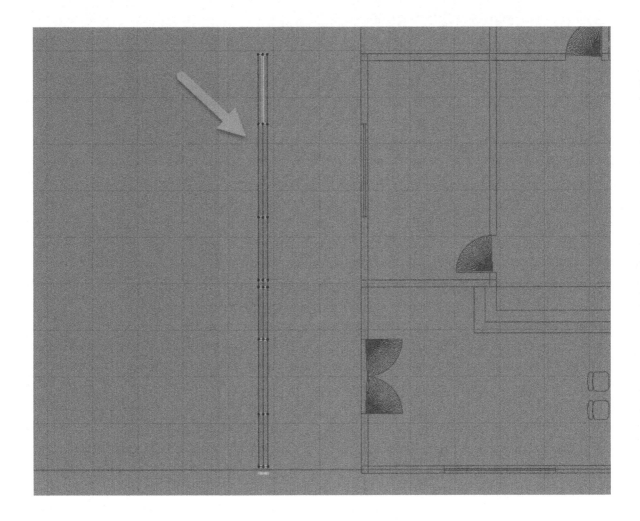

Figure 7.7 - *Dimension line sequence*

As you can see from Figure 7.7, the dimension line object only needs the "Mark FreeStyle Edge" settings. Still in Edit Mode, you can select the central edges and all the horizontal edges from the object and with a right-click, apply the marks. We need those marks to render strokes with the Viewing Collection (Figure 7.8).

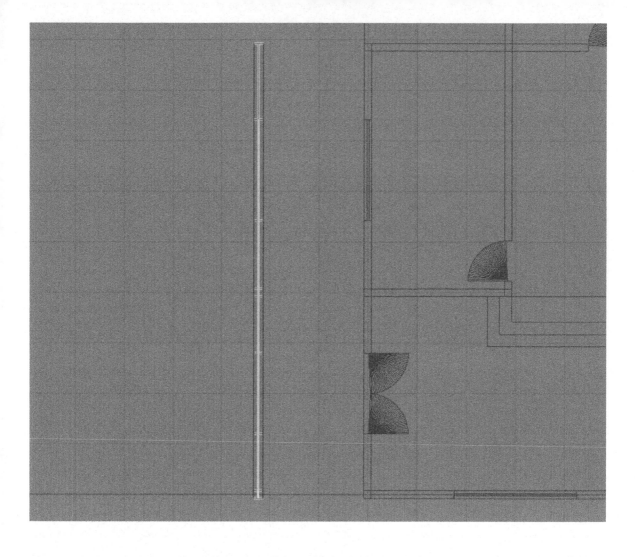

Figure 7.8 - Edges with marks for FreeStyle

After adding the marks to the objects, you will get a complete dimension line on the left side (Figure 7.9).

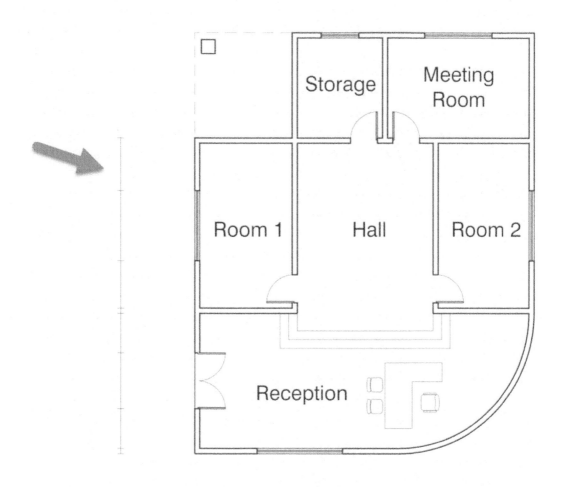

Figure 7.9 - Left side dimension line

You can resize and make adjustments to the dimension lines after having them ready. Keep the Snap During Transform enabled to quickly align the segments to any part of your floor plan or technical drawing.

A single sequence of dimension lines can work as a starting point for all other lines you need in a floor plan or technical drawing. Select the vertices of your dimension line in Edit Mode, and press the SHIFT+D keys. Make a copy of the object in the X-axis and place it to the left (Figure 7.10).

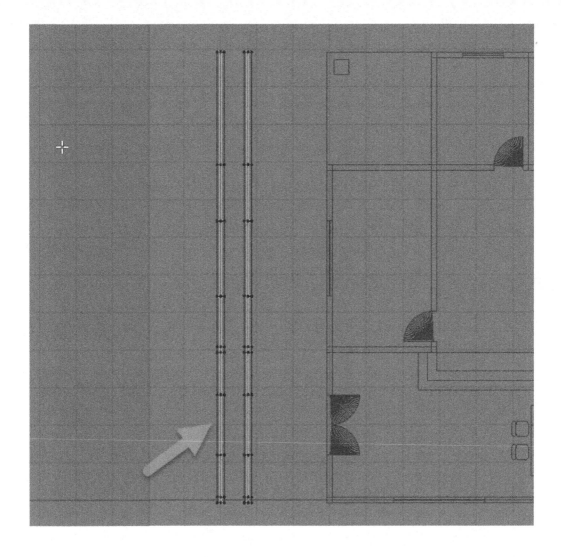

Figure 7.10 - *Copying the dimension line*

From that copy, you can start editing the object to make a single line with no divisions:

1. Press the B key and draw a box to select all internal vertices of your dimension line

2. Press the X key or DELETE and choose Vertices

3. Select four vertices on the left and press the F key

4. Select four vertices on the right and press the F key

You can also replace steps 3-4 with a simple selection of two edges. Change the selection mode to the edge and select a top and bottom edge. Press the F key to connect them with a 3D plane (Figure 7.11).

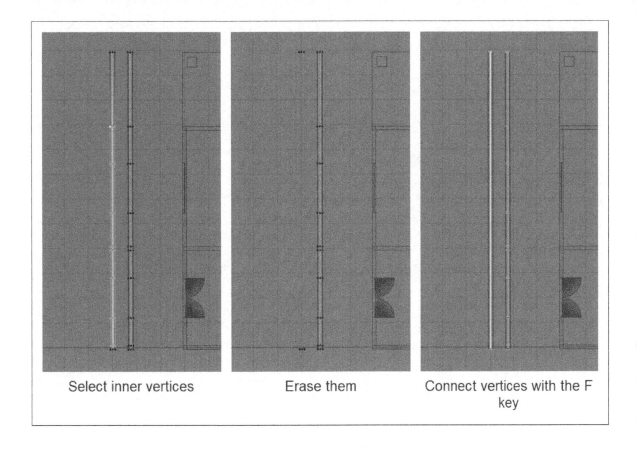

| Select inner vertices | Erase them | Connect vertices with the F key |

Figure 7.11 - *Editing the dimension line*

Select the central edge of that object, and with a right-click open, the Context Menu to add a "Mark FreeStyle Edge." You now have two dimension lines ready for rendering. The next step now is replicating the lines to all other locations you need at the floor plan.

For instance, you can select the lines in Object Mode and press the SHIFT+D keys to duplicate. Add a 90 degrees rotation with the R key to create a horizontal dimension line (Figure 7.12).

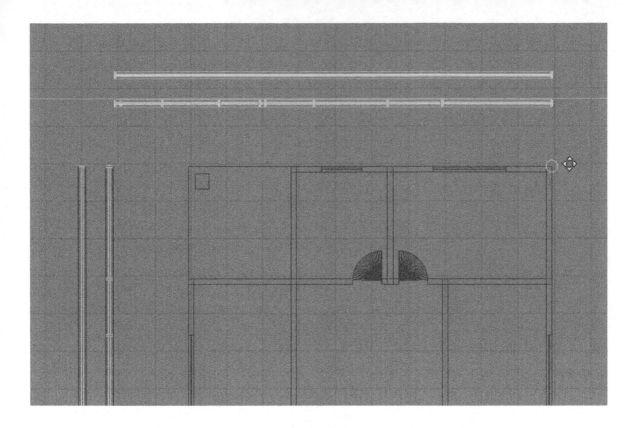

Figure 7.12 - *Copied dimension lines*

Using the same technique, we applied to the first vertical dimension lines, and we can use a combination of the Snap During Transform and the G keys to adjust the lines. Once you have the lines adjusted, it will be necessary to also add the "Mark FreeStyle Edges" to the dimension lines (Figure 7.13).

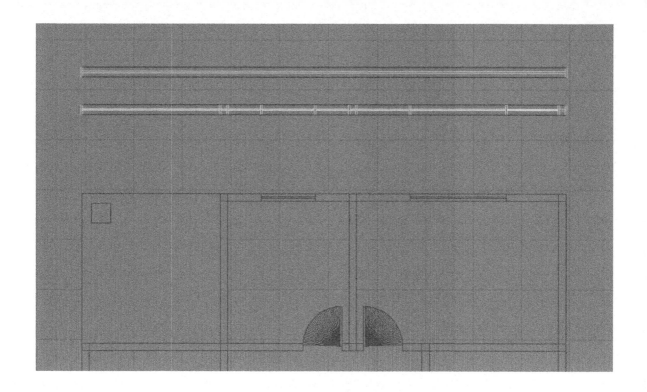

Figure 7.13 - *Horizontal dimension lines*

Select the horizontal dimension lines and press the SHIFT+D keys to duplicate them to the bottom of your floor plan. Repeat the adjustment steps to make each dimension line segment to align with the floor plan (Figure 7.14).

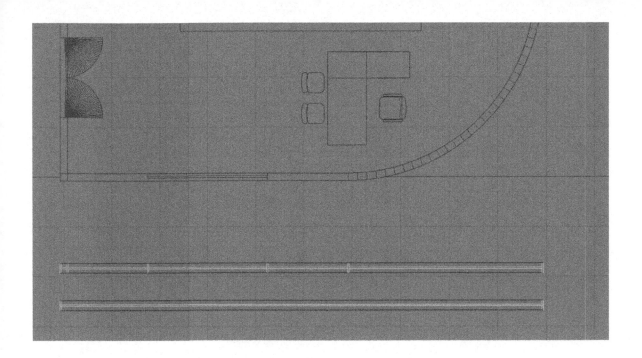

Figure 7.14 - *New horizontal line*

The last dimension line we will need is on the right side of the floor plan. You can use the same steps. Select the dimension lines on the left and press the SHIFT+D key. Make a copy on the X-axis and place them to the left side. Use the "Snap During Transform" to align each segment (Figure 7.15).

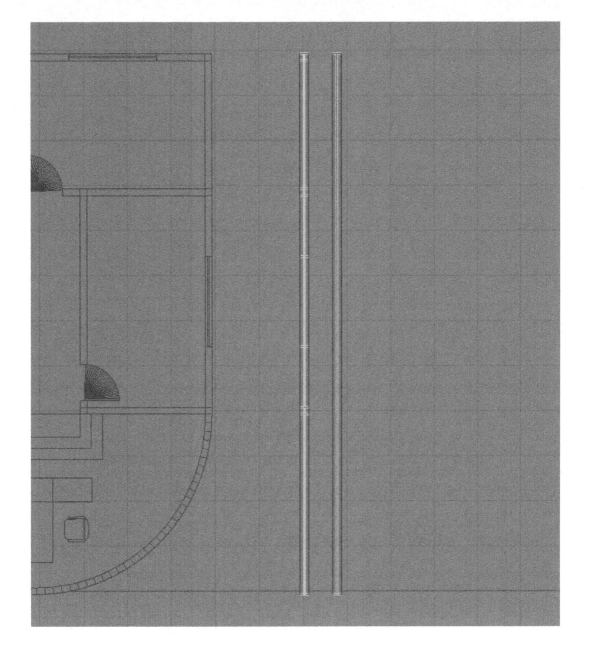

Figure 7.15 - *Last dimension lines*

Once you have all the edge marks applied to the dimension lines, it is time to start a test render. You will see all dimension lines in the floor plan (Figure 7.16).

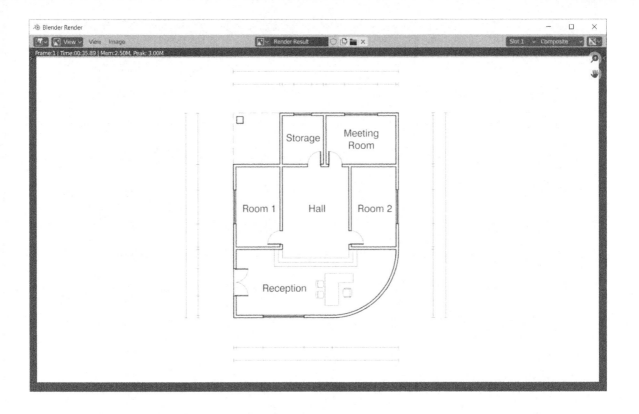

Figure 7.16 - External dimension lines

The only remaining dimension lines we have to create in the floor plan are a couple of lines in the interior of our building.

7.3 Creating internal dimension lines

The creation of interior dimension lines for the floor plan object requires only a duplicate object from any of the existing dimensions. You can select a segment for the dimension lines and press the SHIFT+D keys. Place that new segment close to the wall shown in Figure 7.17.

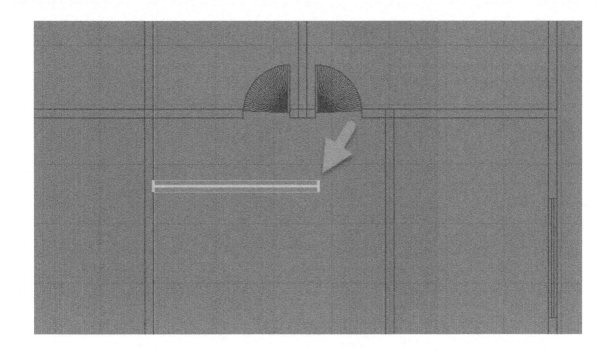

Figure 7.17 - *Copied segment*

Using the extrude tool, you can expand the segment with the help of "Snap During Transform" to align each new segment to the walls. In our case, we need four new extrudes (Figure 7.18).

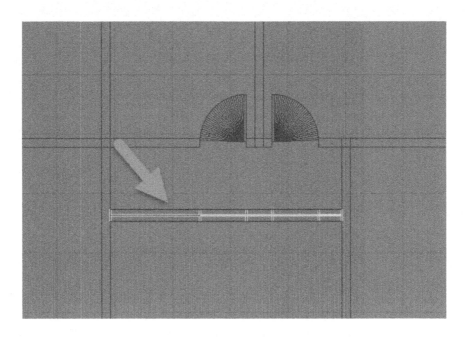

Figure 7.18 - *New segments*

Select any vertical segment from the dimension lines you created and make a copy. Place the copy in the interior of the building, close to the location shown in Figure 7.19.

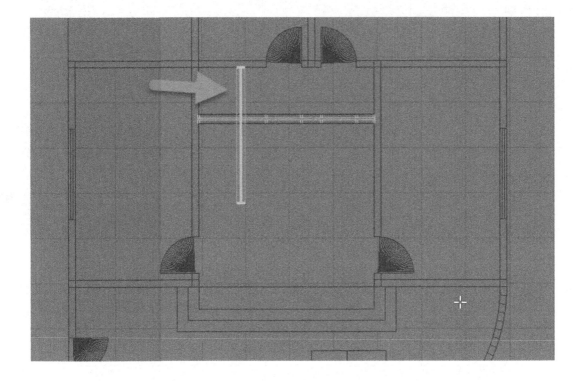

Figure 7.19 - *Vertical segment*

Use the extrude tool again to expand the lines with new segments (Figure 7.20).

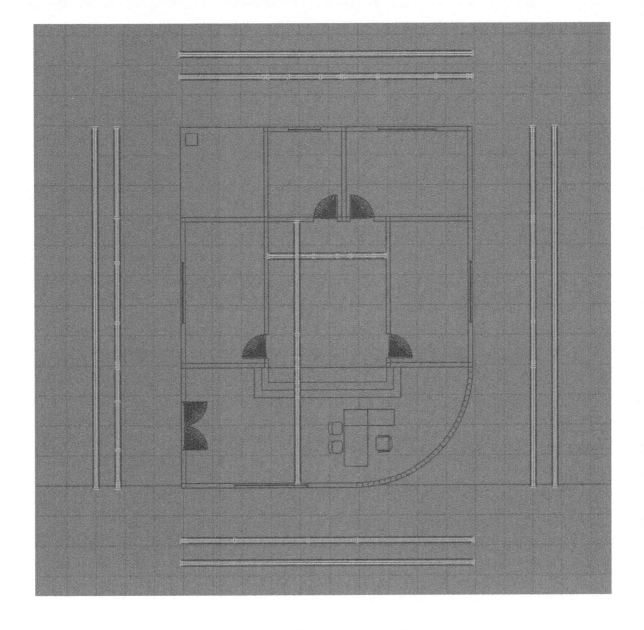

Figure 7.20 - *Expanded dimension lines*

Add the marks to the edges in your dimension lines, and you will have all of them ready to render.

7.4 Adding text to dimension lines

When you start working with dimension lines, you will quickly realize that it doesn't have any feature to help us aligning and placing dimensions at the center of each line. To align each one of the dimension text objects, you will have to use:

- A combination of the G key with either the X or Y keys

- Place the origin point of your text objects at the render of your text, and use the Snap to align it with the 3D Cursor. That will work if you also place the 3D Cursor at the center of each edge from the dimension line

- Use coordinates to place each text object at the center of each segment for a dimension line

No matter the method you choose to align each one of the text objects, you will have to place them in Blender manually.

Another important aspect of the text objects we create for all dimension lines is that they will have to use the "Text" Collection. The same Collection used for the annotations and has a connection to a View Layer capable of rendering solid colors only. To get started, you can press the SHIFT+A keys and add a new text object.

As a way to make text creation faster, you can also get any of the annotations from the floor plan and press SHIFT+D to get a text with all properties we need, like materials and the "Text" Collection (Figure 7.21).

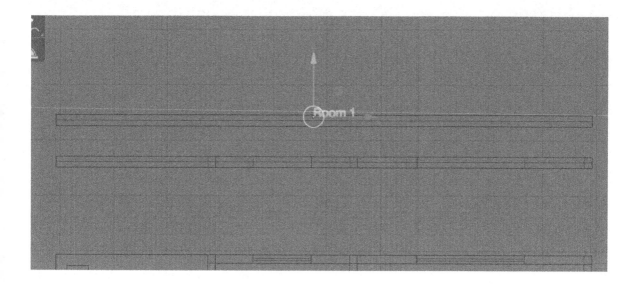

Figure 7.21 - *New text object*

You can enable the display of edge lengths from the Overlays options in Blender, and see each length you must type for a dimension line straight from the edge below. Select the dimension lines and go to Edit Mode and get the edge you want to view the length (Figure 7.22).

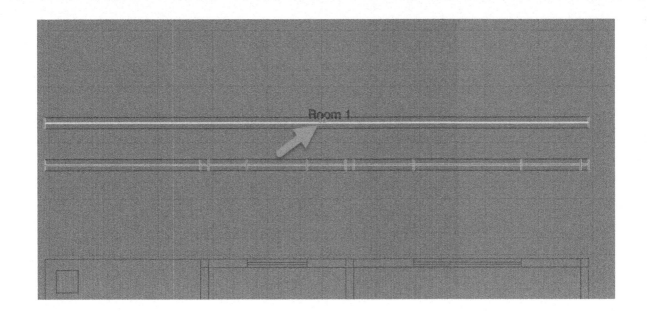

Figure 7.22 - Edge length

From that length, you can select the text object and replace the value with the current dimension (Figure 7.23).

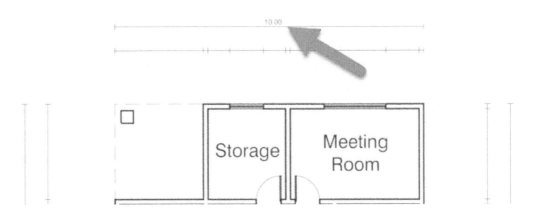

Figure 7.23 - Text with dimension

Using the SHIFT+D keys, you can replicate the text to each one of the dimension lines (Figure 7.24).

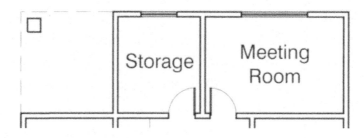

Figure 7.24 - *Copied text object*

The same applied to all other dimension lines in the floor plan object (Figure 7.25). You will have to rotate the text objects to align with the floor plan.

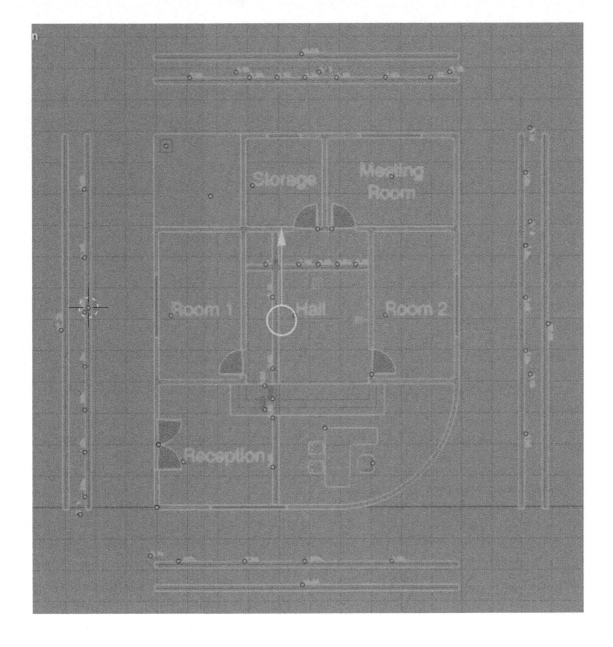

Figure 7.25 - All text objects

If you render the scene with all the text objects related to dimension lines, the floor plan will look like Figure 7.26 shows.

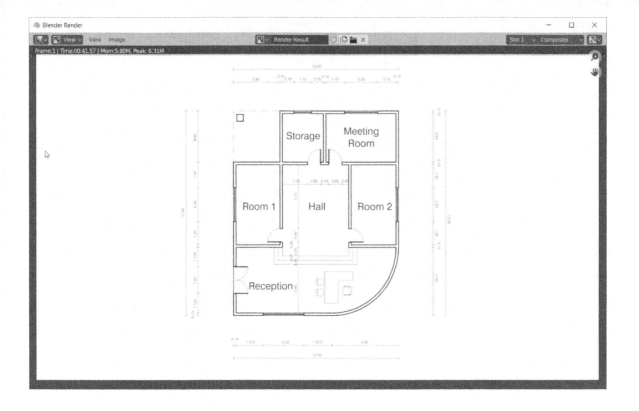

Figure 7.26 - Floor plan with all dimension line text

The only missing information for our floor plan now is the level symbol that will help identify the height of each floor.

Tip: As a way to speed up the dimension lines creation, you can also add the text during the setup of each dimension line. That way all text will already stay in place once you duplicate the dimension lines.

7.5 Creating architectural symbols

Besides having to add dimension lines to a technical drawing, you will also have to create some common symbols to help read your technical drawing. For instance, in architectural drawings like a floor plan, you have something called a level symbol. The symbol helps identify differences on the floor level from a top view.

That symbol usually is a circular object that has two lines crossing and the value for each level appearing above the extension of one of those lines. Using the knowledge we have from FreeStyle and the simple rule about adding strokes to shapes with a 3D face, we can design any symbol for technical drawing.

7.5.1 Making a level symbol

Since the level symbol for architectural drawings has a circle as the main shape, we can start the process of creation, adding a Circle object to the scene. Place the 3D Cursor in a position away from the floor plan. You can replace the 3D Cursor with the mouse. Activate the 3D Cursor button from the Toolbar on the left and click anywhere in your 3D Viewport.

Press the SHIFT+A keys, and from the Mesh group, chooses the Circle option. From the small menu that appears at the bottom left of your screen, you can keep the circle with 32 steps (Figure 7.27).

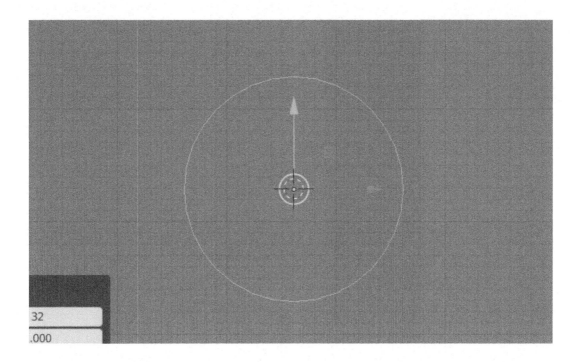

Figure 7.27 - Circle object

Don't work about the scale of your circle yet, because we can adjust that later when you have all objects of the symbol.

Select the Circle object and go to Edit Mode:

1. In Edit Mode, change the selection mode to vertex

2. Press the A key to select all vertices from the Circle

3. Press the E key to extrude all vertices

4. Press the ESC key to cancel your transformation

5. Press the S key to apply a scale

6. Type zero in your keyboard

The main objective with the extrude of your circle with a size of zero is to create several 3D planes that we will use later to add strokes and a solid fill (Figure 7.28).

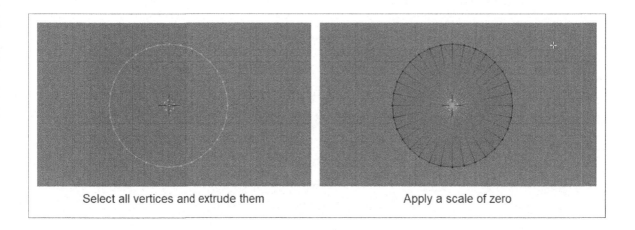

| Select all vertices and extrude them | Apply a scale of zero |

Figure 7.28 - *Extruding the circle vertices*

A level symbol has two lines that cross the main circle and go beyond the circle shape at each side. Only the line on the right has a big extension that will later receive the level value. To create each one of the lines, we have to select two edges on each side and make a small extrude (Figure 7.29).

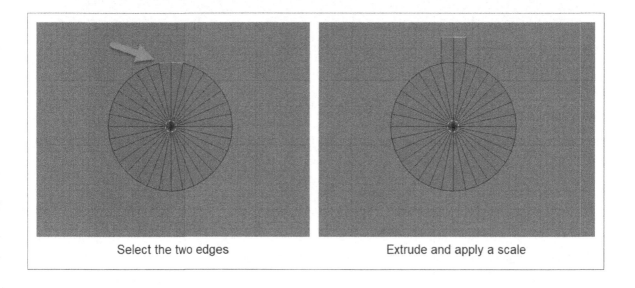

| Select the two edges | Extrude and apply a scale |

Figure 7.29 - *Extrudes to create the top line*

In Edit Mode, you can change the selection mode to the edge and:

1. Select the top two edges from your circle
2. Press the E key
3. Type 0.2
4. Press RETURN to confirm
5. Press the S key
6. Press the Y key
7. Type 0
8. Press RETURN to confirm

Since we are working with two edges coming from a circle, you must apply a scale with a size of zero in the Y-axis to level them. As a result, you will get the two edges making a perfect horizontal line.

You can repeat the same process for the two center edges on the left side of your circle (Figure 7.30).

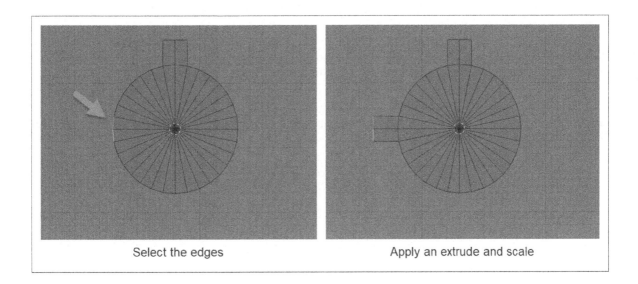

Select the edges	Apply an extrude and scale

Figure 7.30 - *Two edges on the left*

From the sequence of steps to create the extrude, you will have to make two small adjustments:

– Use -0.2 for the extrude size
– The scale for both edges will have to be on the X-axis

The same process will also apply to the two edges on the bottom of your circle (Figure 7.31).

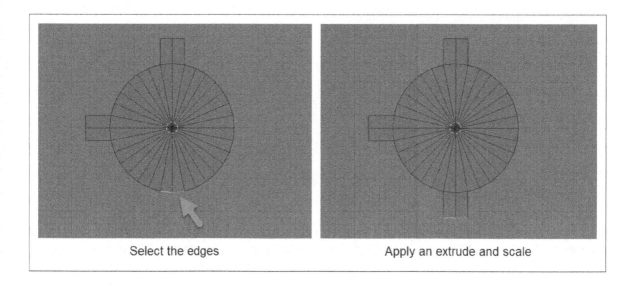

| Select the edges | Apply an extrude and scale |

Figure 7.31 - Edges at the bottom

As for the extrude, you can apply the scale with a size of zero to the Y-axis, but the value used for your extrude will be -0.2. Repeat the same process to the edges on the right side of your circle, but make a larger extrude. A value of 2 will be enough for that extrude and also apply a scale in the X-axis.

Once you have all the extruded edges comes an important part of the design process. A level symbol has four divisions in the circle, where two of those parts will have a solid black fill. To create that solid fill, we must separate the faces into another object.

Still in Edit Mode, change the selection mode to faces and select all faces shown in Figure 7.32.

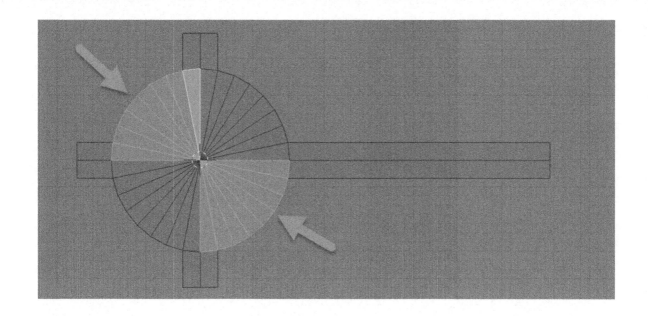

Figure 7.32 - *Selected faces*

After selecting the faces, you can press the P key and choose "Selected" to create a new object-based with all those faces.

To get a solid fill on those faces when rendering, we have to use the same procedure from text objects. In Chapter 6, we created two View Layers for our floor plan. One that has all drawing elements and will only render the strokes from FreeStyle. A second View Layer that has only text objects and will render using a black material and no data from FreeStyle.

Select the object created from those selected faces and move them to the Text Collection (Figure 7.33).

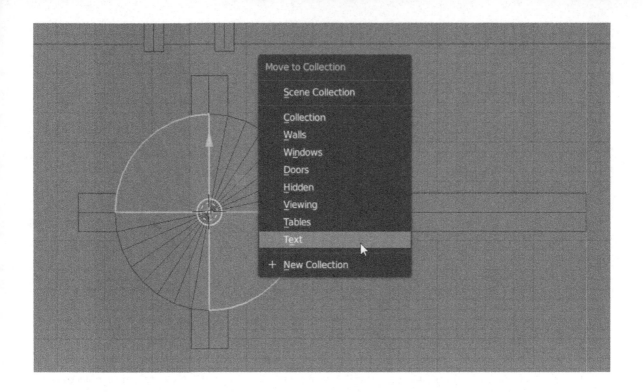

Figure 7.33 - *Text Collection*

Since the Text Collection has a setup to ignore FreeStyle settings in the Text View Layer will get a solid fill color. Also, apply the black material to the object.

Tip: *Remember that before rendering, you should disable the Text Collection from the Drawing View Later. You can quickly enable and disable any Collection from a View Layer with the E key. Select the Collection from the Outliner window and press the E key.*

7.5.2 Adding Edge Marks and Collections

The last step to have our symbol ready to render is adding the proper "Mark FreeStyle Edges" to the places where we need a stroke. Select the edges shown in Figure 7.34.

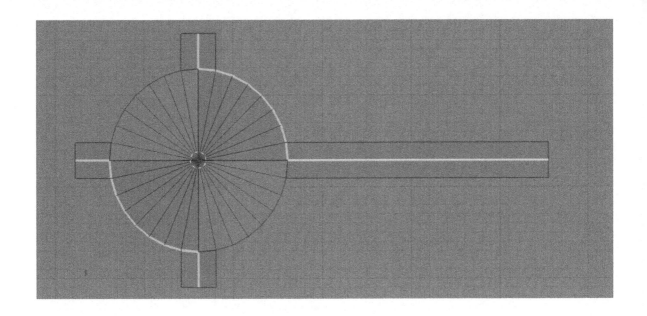

Figure 7.34 - *Selected edges*

With the edges selected, you can open the Context Menu with a right-click and choose "Mark FreeStyle Edge." That will make the edges receive a stroke when rendering. Finally, you can move this object to the Viewing Collection to make it receive the same strokes and settings from that Line Set.

Press the M key and choose the Viewing Collection (Figure 7.35).

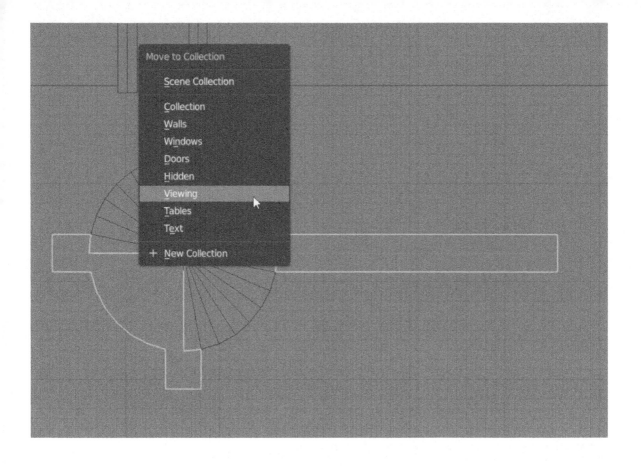

Figure 7.35 - *Move to the Viewing Collection*

We are now ready to render the level symbol. Add a text object that will display the current level for each floor and press F12. In Figure 7.36, you can see the symbol in more detail.

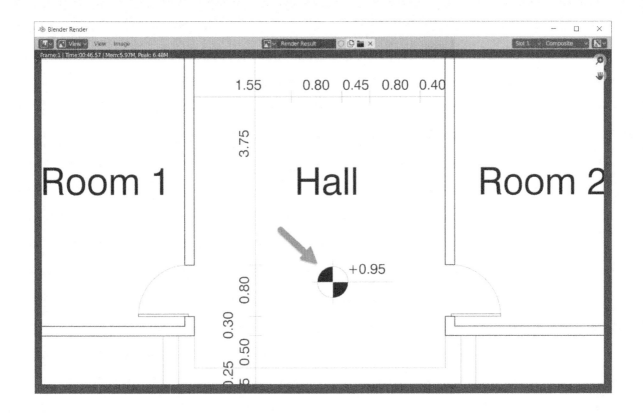

Figure 7.36 - *Level symbol*

That concludes the design for our floor plan that has now most of the features required to present ideas and visually explain a design (Figure 7.37).

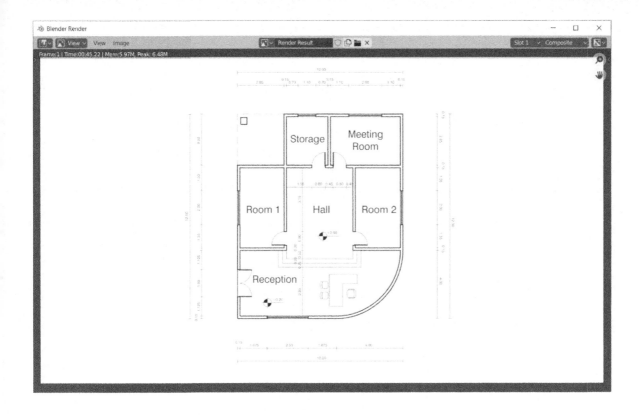

Figure 7.37 - *Floor plan*

You can either save the floor plan drawing using a format like PNG in the Render Window to share and prepare the object for print. Another option that will give much more flexibility regarding technical drawing is to save it as a vector. In Chapter 8, you will learn how to export a render from FreeStyle to a format like SVG.

What is next?

If you had to choose one aspect of the design process in Blender for technical drawing that should receive an upgrade is the dimension lines. Having to align and place dimension lines manually will take a tremendous amount of time and effort, especially in the text alignment process.

As a way to streamline the production, you can start making assets for dimension lines in Blender for later reuse. Create a good number of dimension lines with a fixed design and text objects placed in strategic locations. When you have to create new technical drawings, you can Append those designs to the new project and save some production time.

Create an asset library with various designs of dimension lines to speed up your designs. That is your next step.

Chapter 8 - Isometric cameras and SVG export

Until this chapter, we worked with a type of view to produce technical drawings, which was an orthographic visualization from the top of a drawing. It is now time to make another type of render from objects using an isometric render. In Blender, you can apply settings to a camera that will allow you to make isometric renders from any object.

Besides the camera, we can also use options from the Line Set on FreeStyle to render hidden faces from 3D models using dashed lines. That will help you create a popular type of visualization for projects that need a perspective view of any object with no distortions from the camera.

And to finish our book, you will learn how to save technical renders from Blender as vectors using the SVG file format.

Here is a list of what you will learn:

- Rendering hidden lines

- Creating an Isometric render

- Making four isometric cameras

- Rendering to SVG

- Saving SVG files

- Working with multiple cameras

8.1 Rendering hidden lines

After we finished the floor plan drawing in the last chapter, you probably have a great idea about the workflow required to create 2D drawings in Blender. The basic workflow involves the "drawing" of a bidimensional object that we will render like if it was a drawing coming from a CAD tool. From that same model, you can later create a full-featured 3D visualization with either Cycles or Eevee.

However, another kind of technical drawing takes 3D objects that will render with a unique set of features. For instance, you will get a volume that should display hidden faces with dashed lines.

That type of technical drawing is common in fields such as mechanical drawing and design. In those projects, you will also display the object using an isometric perspective and not an orthographic view from the top.

In Blender, we can easily create such type of render using a feature of FreeStyle that we still didn't use until now. To describe how we can use those features and create an isometric view of an object, we can use a simple model like the one shown in Figure 8.1.

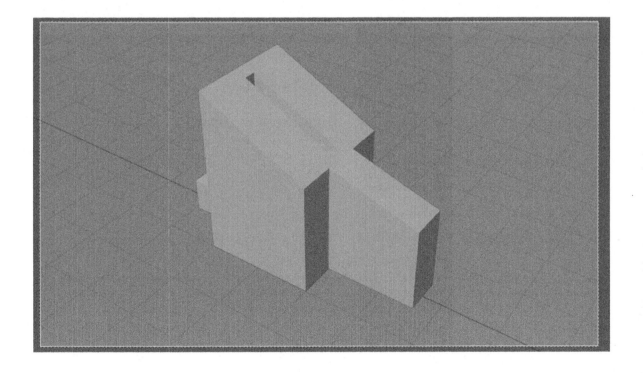

Figure 8.1 - 3D Shape to render

If you enable FreeStyle and make a Line Set for the object with all default options, you will get a render with only the borders (Figure 8.2).

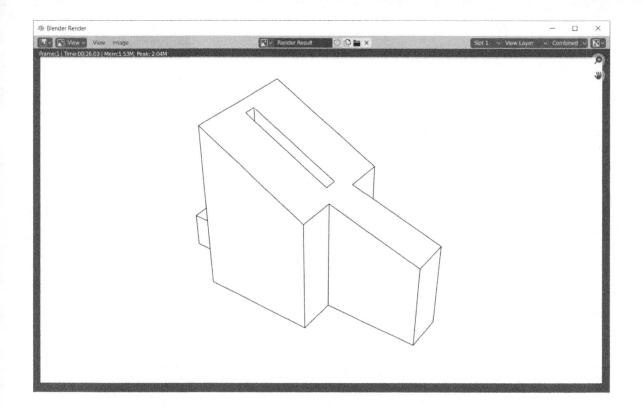

Figure 8.2 - Render with default settings

To get that render, we followed the same settings used in previous chapters:

1. Choose Cycles as the main renderer

2. At the Filter options disable the Surface

3. Set the background with a white color

4. Change the settings in the Color Management to get a plain white color

What if we wanted to also display and render all hidden lines from the 3D model? To also render all hidden lines from the object, you will have to create two unique Line Sets. The first Line Set, which you can rename to "Visible" will store all the settings for visible lines (Figure 8.3).

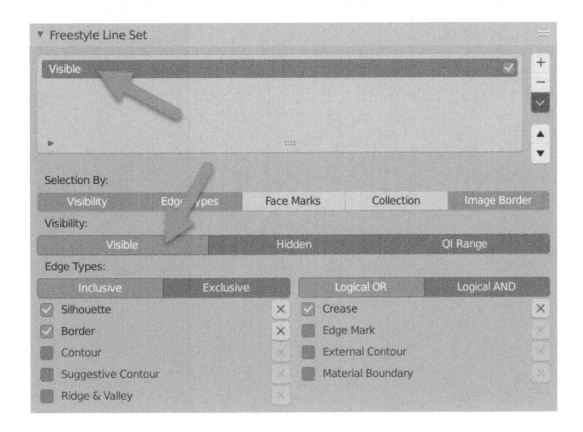

Figure 8.3 - *Visible Line Set*

Notice that in the default options for a Line Set, you will find a field called "Visibility." One of the options there will set the type of edge you want to render with that Line Set. It will always start with the "Visible" button enabled.

To render hidden lines in a 3D model, you can create a new Line Set in the list and rename that as "Hidden" (Figure 8.4).

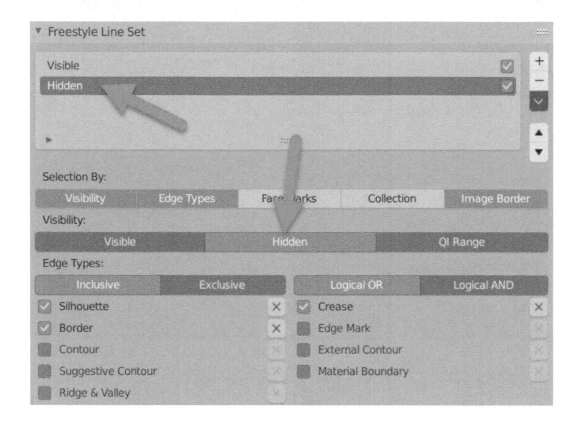

Figure 8.4 - *Hidden Line Set*

At the Visibility options from that Line Set, you will choose the "Hidden" option. That will make it identify and process all hidden borders and objects. With that Line Set selected go to the Line Style options.

For the Line Style, you can choose a unique name like "hidden" to help you identify the purpose of that style. For the Line Style, enable the "Dashed Line" option and use values of 10 and 5 for the dashes and gap, respectively (Figure 8.5).

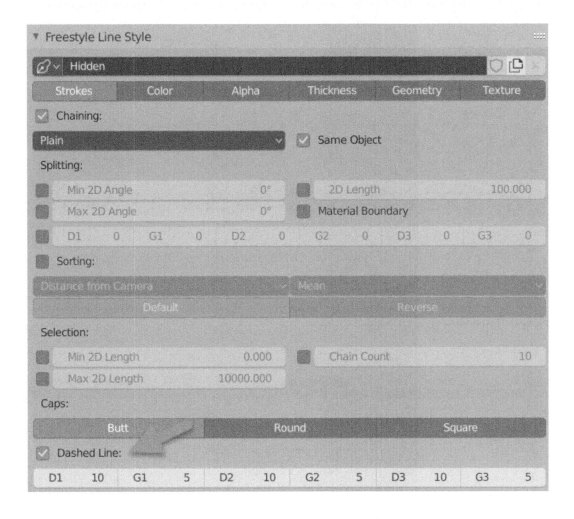

Figure 8.5 - *Hidden Line Style*

In a technical drawing, the lines that are usually hidden will appear with a thinner line style. Go to the Thickness options and change the value of that line thickness to 1.0000 (Figure 8.6).

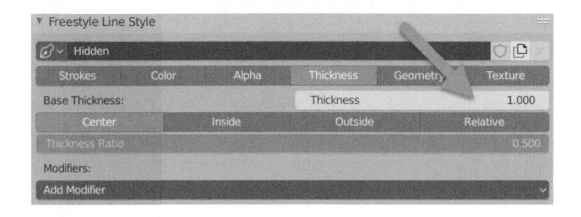

Figure 8.6 - Thickness settings

The Line Style that renders all strokes from the Visible Line Set has a default thickness of 3, which will be visually different from the dashed lines. If you render the object now, you will see all hidden faces appearing with dashed lines (Figure 8.7).

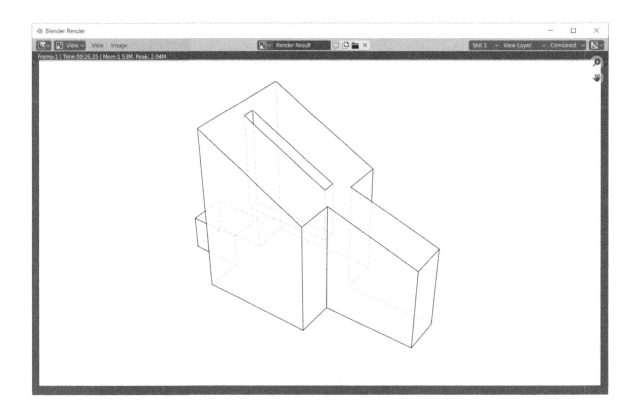

Figure 8.7 - Render with hidden objects

By rendering hidden objects with a dashed line, you can create all types of technical visualization. For instance, you can create a technical visualization of a motor engine or the design of a product that has internal parts. The possibilities are endless.

When rendering dashed lines from FreeStyle, you should keep in mind that the values for dashes and gaps will depend on the scale of your 3D model and render. For instance, in the previous render, we used values of 10 and 5 for both dashed and gaps. Depending on the size and scale of your model, you might have to use higher or lower values.

If you try to render dashes and they still appear as a solid continuous line, you will probably have to reduce the sizes.

Tip: For complex objects that have multiple shapes and also parts, you can also use Collections to organize the project and the "Mark FreeStyle Edges" to control which objects will receive a stroke. If you decide to use such features, it will be necessary to make the proper adjustments to the Line Set settings.

8.2 Creating an Isometric render

The camera used to render our object from the last section looks like an isometric camera, but it doesn't have the right settings. An isometric visualization of any object is common in technical drawings when you want to show an object without the distortions of a perspective projection.

An isometric render will help you better understand a design because it offers a view of the object with correct proportions. If you decide to print the visualization to paper, you can even get a scale to take measurements from the 3D representation.

In Blender, we can create an isometric camera by selecting the camera object you want to use and open the Object Properties. There you will see all options regarding object transformations (Figure 8.8).

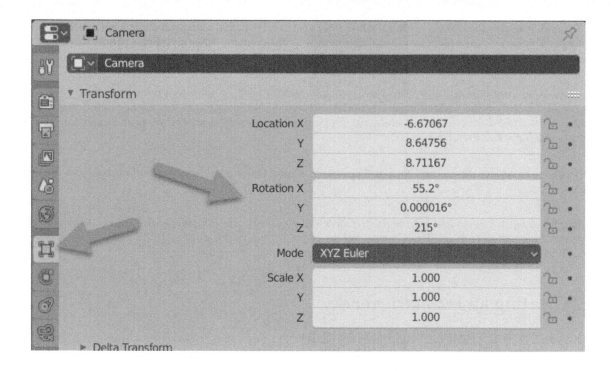

Figure 8.8 - Object properties for camera

To make an isometric view of any scene using a camera in Blender, we have to change the Rotation settings. From all the three-axis, you can change, the most important is the X-axis rotation. You must set the rotation for the X-axis with a value of 60 degrees.

As for the other values, we can use zero for the Y-axis and imagine you want a view of the object from a "corner" location we can rotate it in the Z-axis using values such as:

– 45

– 135

– 225

– 315

Later we will see an example of how those angles will affect the camera location and point of view. Besides working with the rotation, you should also change the projection type of your camera to Orthographic (Figure 8.9).

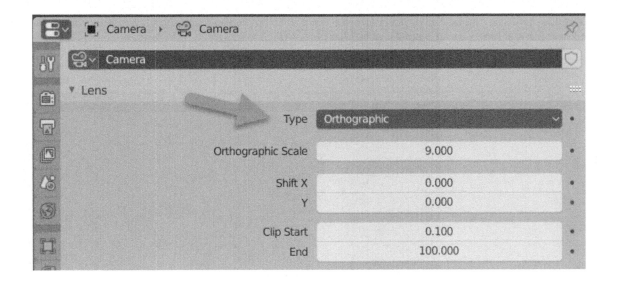

Figure 8.9 - *Camera Type*

In theory, you will start to see the objects at the 3D Viewport with an isometric view (Figure 8.10).

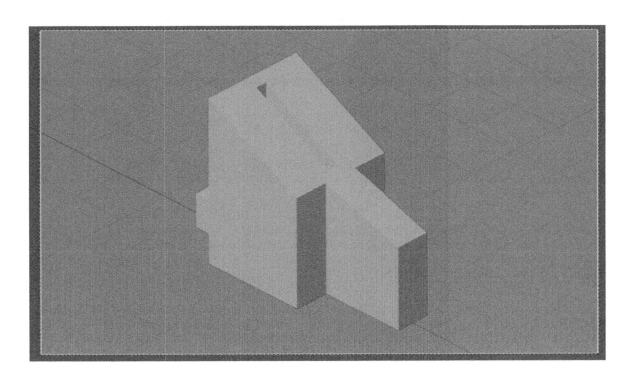

Figure 8.10 - *Isometric view from 3D Viewport*

A render will also display the objects with an isometric visualization using the same settings we already used to create the Line Sets for visible and hidden objects (Figure 8.11).

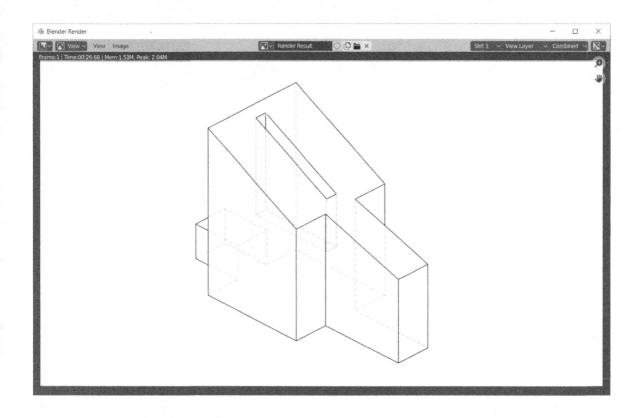

Figure 8.11 - Isometric render

It all appears to be working great until you take that image and tries to match with other isometric visualizations created with other tools. The 3D camera from Blender will create a small distortion from an isometric rendering like the one we are trying to create.

The distortion is small enough to pass unnoticed at the naked eye. Still, you can take the results of the render and import it to a graphical application and try to measure the angles each line makes with both horizontal and vertical axis. An isometric drawing will have the objects making an angle of 30 degrees, and those renders do not match that angle.

Tip: Once you have an isometric camera in Blender, you will change the framing by using the G key as usual. But, instead of making a free movement with the mouse, you will try to constrain all camera moves to the X or Y-axis. Press the Numpad 0 to see your active camera and select it by clicking at the border. Press the G key and either the Y or X keys.

8.2.1 Settings for a true isometric camera

To fix the distortion problem found in the 3D Camera and create a true isometric visualization of any problem, we must use another value for the X-axis rotation of your camera. Instead of using 60 degrees for the rotation, you should use "54.736" as the value (Figure 8.12).

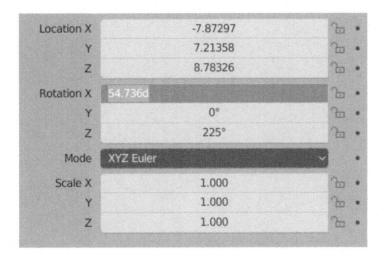

Figure 8.12 - Fixed rotation

If you use that value as the rotation for the camera, you will get a slightly different angle for the object at the render, but all values will match an isometric perspective (Figure 8.13).

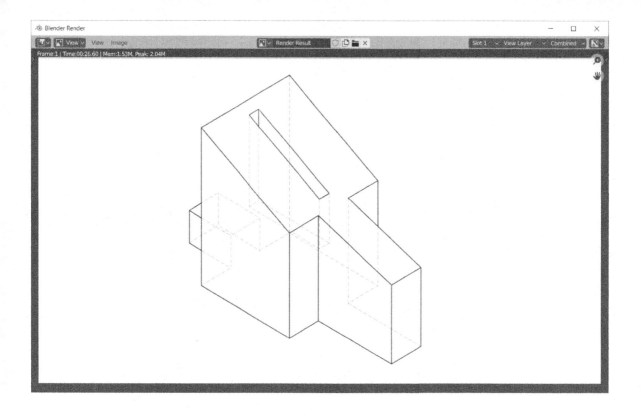

Figure 8.13 - Perspective with fixed values

That same isometric camera will help you create images that will match with other objects that also use the same type of visualization.

Info: The distortion of an orthographic camera to render isometric perspectives is not a "problem" of Blender. You will find the same recommendations regarding camera angle rotations for lots of other 3D tools.

8.3 Making four isometric cameras

One of the benefits of using Blender to create isometric perspectives is that you can make multiple cameras and render different views from any object. For instance, you can place an object in a plane and make a camera that will stay at each corner of that plane.

For instance, we can get the camera from our last section that is using has all the values to render a true isometric view of any object and make duplicates. Assuming you are starting with a camera that has values for rotation such as:

 – **X**: 54.736

 – **Y**: 0

– **Z**: 225

That camera will create a render from the northwest location of an orthographic plane. To have a better visualization of your scene, you can change the viewing angle to the top using the Numpad 7. Select the camera and press SHIFT+D to make a copy. Press the X key to move the camera on the X-axis and place it to the right.

For that camera, you should use the following rotation settings:

 – **X**: 54.736

 – **Y**: 0

 – **Z**: 135

With that rotation, you will get a camera viewing the scene from the northeast. Select the two cameras from the scene and duplicate them on the Y-axis and place them to the bottom of your scene. For the camera in the lower right corner, you can use the following rotation values:

 – **X**: 54.736

 – **Y**: 0

 – **Z**: 45

The camera will view the scene from the southeast. Select the camera in the bottom left and change the rotation to:

 – **X**: 54.736

 – **Y**: 0

 – **Z**: 315

If you follow all the procedures, you will have a scene that has four cameras capable of rendering isometric perspectives from any object you place in the scene (Figure 8.14).

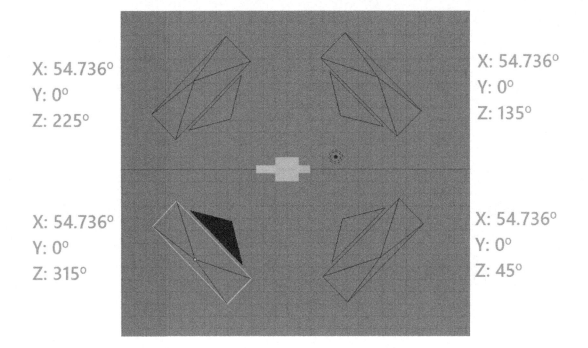

X: 54.736°
Y: 0°
Z: 225°

X: 54.736°
Y: 0°
Z: 135°

X: 54.736°
Y: 0°
Z: 315°

X: 54.736°
Y: 0°
Z: 45°

Figure 8.14 - *Isometric camera locations*

You can quickly render different views from a project using those cameras by selecting them and making each one active for render. For instance, you can select a camera and press CTRL+Numpad 0 to make the camera active. Press F12 to render that camera.

In Figure 8.15, you can see a composition of all four renders coming from those cameras.

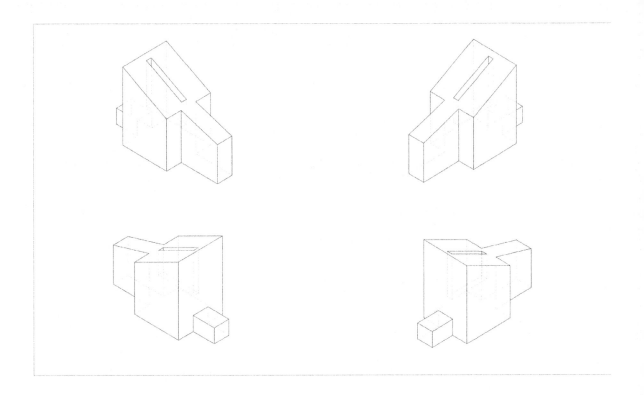

Figure 8.15 - *Isometric views composition*

You can quickly create those renders in Blender using each available camera in a scene.

Working with isometric cameras in Blender will require you some adaptation from the usual perspective projection. If you want to keep the images coming from multiple cameras consistent, you should avoid making changes to the orthographic scale of a single camera.

Whenever you have to change the settings for a single camera, the same option must replica to all others to keep the images with the same scale and settings. Another aspect of an isometric camera that you will have to adjust is the framing. After making the camera duplicates, you must adjust the framing:

1. Select the camera you want to adjust

2. Press the CTRL+Numpad 0 to make it active

3. Select the camera border

4. Press the G key

5. Press either the X or Y keys

6. Move the mouse cursor to adjust framing

7. Left-click with the mouse to confirm the framing

Once you have the camera with good framing, you can repeat the same process in all others. Making the camera copies from the top view will not ensure you have good framing for them.

8.4 Rendering to SVG

Until this point in the book, we made several different renders to create technical drawings based on 2D and 3D objects. You can save those renders in formats such as PNG that will work great for the web and also print. Even with a lot of features such as a compression that keep most of the image information and the ability to have a transparent background, you will find some limitations in the PNG format.

Despite all the features from a PNG file, it is still an image that has pixels as the main building block. Like many other formats that also use pixels as the main technique to form images, you will find that working with scaling could add significant distortions to the file.

For instance, if you render a technical drawing in Blender and save it as a PNG file with a resolution of 1000x500 pixels, and later you discover that you need the image with the two times more pixels, you will have to render it again. By taking that same image and applying a scale, you will end up with a pixelation effect for all lines in the image.

If you want a better option to output technical drawing from Blender, you can also render the lines in a vector format. From FreeStyle, we can render projects using the SVG file format. By using a vector format, you can freely change the scaling and sizes without any distortions.

Unlike an image that has fixed pixels as the base, a vector file has a bath in math coordinates that will refresh every time you try to read or display the file. Regardless of the size, you want to view the lines; they will maintain the same quality without any visible distortions.

8.4.1 Saving SVG files

To save your technical drawing renders as vectors, you have to enable the SVG exporter in Blender. The exporter is available in Blender as an Add-on that, by default, will come disabled. Go to the Edit → Preferences menu and open the Add-ons tab. There you can type SVG in the search box to see that Add-on (Figure 8.16).

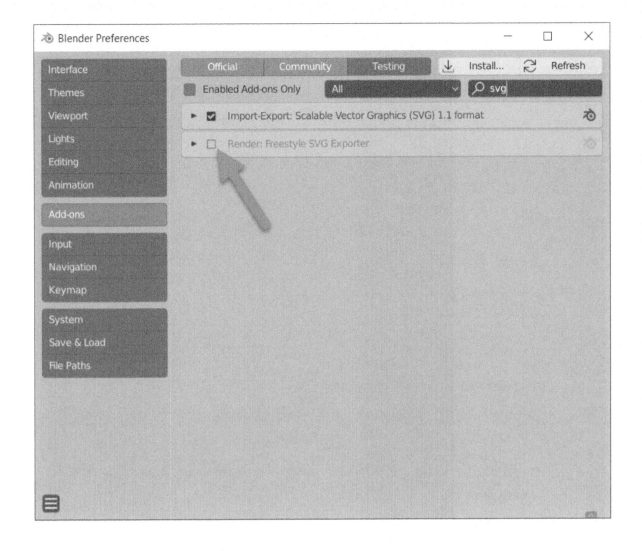

Figure 8.16 - SVG Exporter Add-on

Enable the Add-on, and you will be able to save any render from FreeStyle as an SVG file. After you enable the Add-on, new options will appear in the Render Properties tab (Figure 8.17).

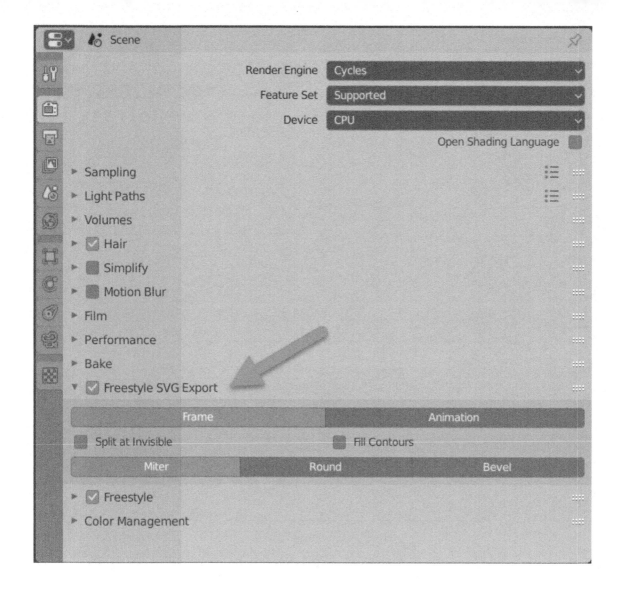

Figure 8.17 - *SVG Exporter settings*

You must enable the exporter there to create vector files from your projects. Besides the SVG exporter options at the Render Properties, you will also find settings at the View Layer Properties (Figure 8.18).

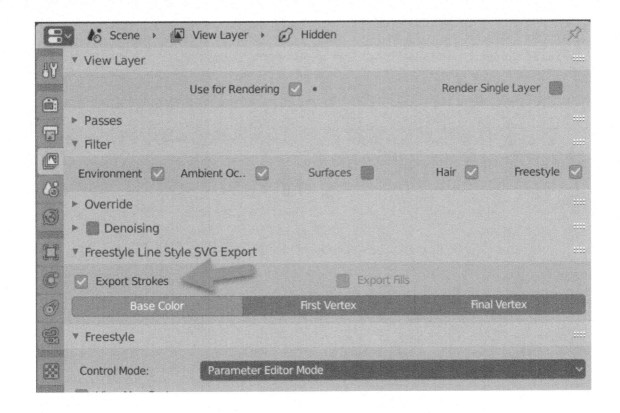

Figure 8.18 - *View Layer properties*

At the View Layer options, you should enable the "Export Strokes" option to make all your strokes become vector lines in the SVG file.

After you have all the settings for an SVG file saved, it is time to start rendering the project. Unlike a PNG file that you can save from the Render output window using the Image menu, an SVG file must go straight to a folder in your hard drive or local network. You can choose the place where you will save the SVG file in the Output field of your Render properties (Figure 8.19).

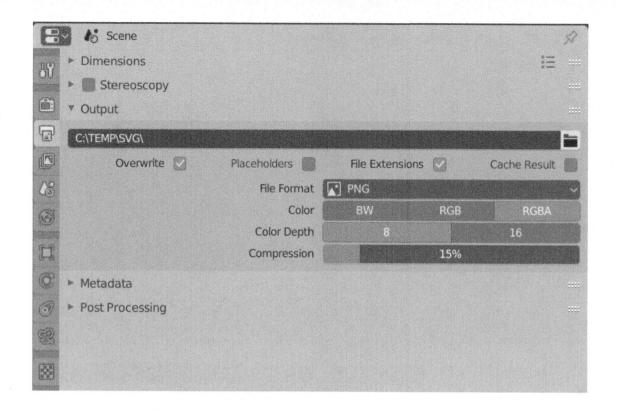

Figure 8.19 - Output field

There you will point the folder where Blender will create the SVG files from any project you try to render. When you press the F12 key to render the project, it will appear in the Render Window and also go to that folder as an SVG file.

Once you start to render projects in SVG, the folder you choose at the Output field will receive SVG files (Figure 8.20).

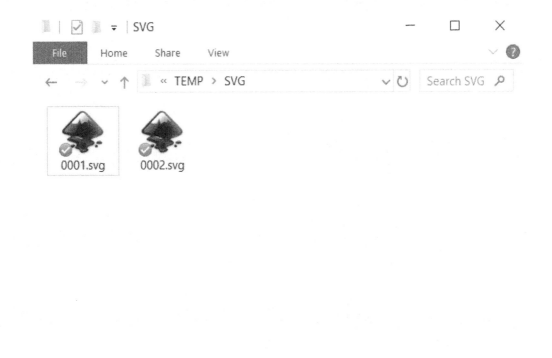

Figure 8.20 - *SVG files*

You can get any of those SVG and import in graphical applications such as Inkscape to edit and manipulate vectors (Figure 8.21).

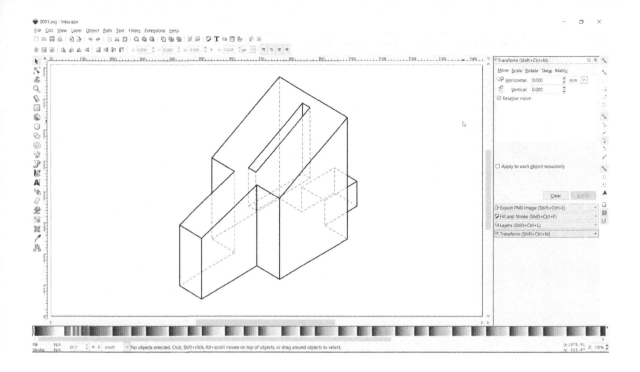

Figure 8.21 - *Render from Blender in Inkscape*

Since Inkscape edits SVG files by default, you can open the Blender generated files there directly.

Tip: You can use Inkscape or any other graphical application to create files for print coming from Blender. For instance, in Inkscape, you will work in a print layout using a paper sheet as the base. With a vector drawing, you can scale and adjust settings in any way you like and create PDF files for print.

8.4.2 Working with multiple cameras

If you decide to start making SVG files from your renders in Blender using the exporter, you will quickly notice that it will create all renders based on the current frame you have in Blender. The SVG exporter can work for both still images and also animations, and if you take a look back at Figure 8.17, you will see that we can render either a Frame or Animation.

For technical drawing, you will most likely render a Frame for still images. How to find the current animation frame in Blender? At the Blender interface, you will see various locations that will show the current animation frame (Figure 8.22).

268

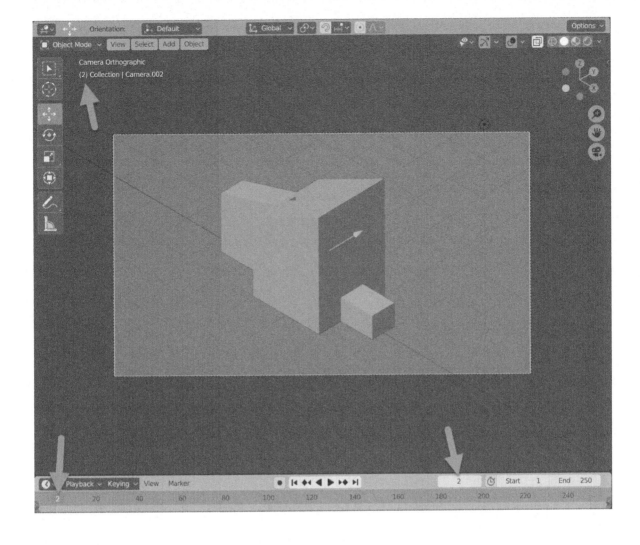

Figure 8.22 - *Current animation frame locations*

When you have to render a single image for a project, you won't have to worry about the current frame of your animation because the exporter will create only a single file. The files will have the number of your current frame like:

- 0001.svg

- 0002.svg

- 0003.svg

In projects where you have multiple cameras to render, like the isometric views we created earlier in the chapter, the current will matter a lot more. By leaving the current frame as always 1 will make the SVG exporter override the "0001.svg" file every time you start a render. To avoid losing the renders, you must change the current frame.

You can easily change the current frame of Blender with the left and right arrow keys from your keyboard:

- **Right arrow**: Go to the next frame

- **Left arrow**: Go to the previous frame

To render multiple cameras, you can choose one camera and make sure you are in frame 1. Press the F12 key to save your render file as "0001.svg" in the folder pointed at the Output field. Once you finish that render, make another camera active and use the Right arrow from your keyboard to change the current frame to 2. Press the F12 again to save the render as "0002.svg".

In Figure 8.20, you can see an example of multiple outputs from cameras. The frame number will be the filename used to create your SVG. Once you have multiple renders, you can also import them to Inkscape to create a print layout (Figure 8.23).

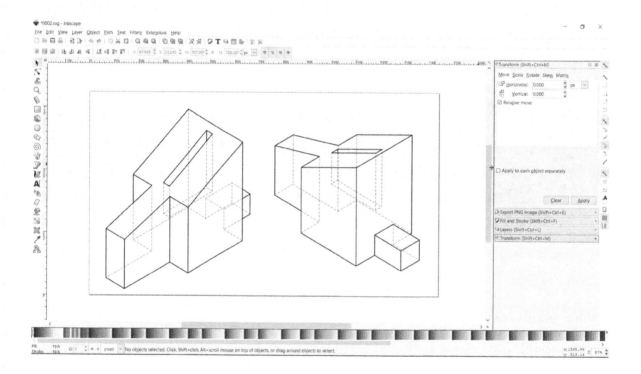

Figure 8.23 - Multiple views in Inkscape

It is possible to edit and manipulate SVG files in multiple applications and not only in Inkscape. You can even view SVG files in some web browsers. An advantage of Inkscape is that it is also a free and open-source like Blender. You can download it from the Inkscape website: https://www.inkscape.org.

What is next?

One of the best features from Blender and FreeStyle is the ability to export your technical drawings in a vector format such as SVG. From that format, you can easily start working with technical drawings for print output. You can import the files in softwares like Inkscape and also use any compatible vector application like Illustrator or Affinity Designer.

Regardless of the platform, you choose to edit and process the files having the projects saved as an SVG will give you incredible creative power. You can even adjust the scale of your drawings for print in larger formats.

As a next step, you can try to render the floor plan as an SVG file and import it to your preferred vector application. There you can adjust the scale for print and use large paper formats such as A0 or A1 to make a print layout.

Review and rating

Do you like the book content? Don't forget about rating and writing a small review in the Amazon Store where you bought the book. That will help us improve the content and also other readers looking to produce technical drawings with Blender 2.8.

This is an independent production from Blender 3D Architect, which is a site that promotes the use of Blender for architectural visualization.

If you have any questions or comments about the book, you can contact us here:

`https://www.blender3darchitect.com/contact/`

Thank you for your support.

Made in the USA
Coppell, TX
17 July 2020